I0416823

TABLE OF CONTENTS

ILLUSTRATIONS

FIGURES

TABLES

INTRODUCTION

***The battle is fought and decided by quartermasters before the shooting begins.*[1]**
-Field Marshal Erwin Rommel

On 4 April 2004, Al Qaeda-in-Iraq (AQ-I) conducted a series of well coordinated

attacks on eight key bridges and several sections of Allied main and alternate supply

routes across the breadth of Iraq. These near simultaneous attacks resulted in damaged

supply routes with seven of the eight bridges (all located at critical, otherwise

inaccessible, points along their respective routes) destroyed and several military service

members and contractors killed. These attacks, combined with the ambush and grisly

killing of four contractors in Fallujah five days earlier, had a devastating effect on the

U.S. military's relationship with its largest defense contractor in the region, and a

subsequent negative effect on the American military's ability to sustain itself.[2]

For the first time since the Department of Defense began its widespread use of

logistics and sustainment contractors during military operations in the Balkans almost a

decade earlier, contractors blinked and hesitated in the execution of their duties. These

devastating insurgent attacks in what previously were believed to be U.S. "controlled"

areas combined with the deliberate targeting of U.S. defense contractors to cause the

largest single logistics/sustainment contracting firm in the region to question whether its

lucrative contract with the U.S. government was worth the potential serious injury or

death of its employees. Despite being hired to conduct operational level sustainment

functions for a combat force, the contractor suspended operations for several days until

---

[1] Erwin Johannes Eugen Rommel, *The Rommel Papers,* ed. B.H. Liddell Hart (New York: Harcourt, Brace and Company, 1953), 328.

[2] First hand author account. At the time of the event described, the author was deployed in support of Operation IRAQI FREEDOM as a brigade level support operations officer within the 13th Corps Support Command (now called the 13th Expeditionary Sustainment Command), Fort Hood, Texas.

1

the U.S. military developed more stringent combat logistics patrol (logistics convoy) security procedures and increased military-to-contractor combat logistics patrol force ratios. Additionally, many of the contractor's employees quit, causing further delay in the resumption of contracted logistics support. In the meantime, Soldiers, Marines, and in some cases, Airmen and Sailors, put aside their "normal" duties and climbed into cabs of contracted civilian semi tractor-trailer trucks in order to deliver supplies and services to the approximately 130,000 United States military personnel in Iraq. Although military forces accomplished this operational level sustainment mission *in extremis,* they did so at the expense of pulling Army and Marine Infantrymen from their tactical mission of patrolling villages. Indeed, at the tactical (and perhaps operational) level in Iraq, there were no "extra" U.S. service members to take the place of civilian contractors who were unable or unwilling to sustain the fight. Every Soldier, Marine, Airman, and Sailor in Iraq had a primary mission to perform. Secretary of Defense Rumsfeld's transformation agenda and parsimonious authorization of deployment orders guaranteed there were not enough troops to begin with, let alone "extra" troops to backfill missing contractors. Thus, any Soldier, Marine, Airman, or Sailor driving a fuel tanker or riding shotgun was one less man patrolling a village, maintaining an aircraft, loading ordnance, or jamming the remote detonation signal for an improvised explosive device. While the U.S. military adjusted tolerably to the exigencies of a war without a traditionally secure rear area, it has yet to appreciate the greater strategic vulnerability created by an overreliance on contracted logistics and sustainment in a combat zone. Overreliance upon contractors for sustainment is a risk that the military cannot afford to take.

According to American economist and social commentator Thorstein Veblen, "The outcome of any serious research can only be to make two questions grow where only one grew before."[3] Such is the case with this thesis. Initial inquiries sought to prove that the United States military traded logistics force structure for additional combat (maneuver) brigades. However, the data does not support this premise. Personnel figures provided by the U.S. Army for the last twenty years indicate that, as a percentage of the total active force, Army logistics units increased from 18% in FY90 to 23% in FY10.[4] This increase notwithstanding, civilian logistics contractors are a reality on the modern battlefield--the product of an ill-conceived force management policy that perpetuates the belief that "contractors are the answer to the logistics question." This contractors-centric emphasis has resulted in the degradation of the military's logistics and sustainment capability to the point where supporting a large-scale ground combat force is a questionable proposition. This transfer of logistics/sustainment responsibility has had an adverse affect on the U.S. military's ability to support a theater opening force, particularly in a non-permissive hybrid conflict environment. Despite the vast array of military strength on display since October 2001, the uniformed-to-contracted logistics ratio is well out of balance and relies too heavily on contractors who, given the extreme danger of some environments, may not always show up for work. Simply put, when it comes to sustaining ground maneuver forces in a large-scale (Desert Storm equivalent) conflict, the U.S. Military is severely limited and at the mercy of a contracted

---

[3] Thorstein Veblen, "The Evolution of the Scientific Point of View." *The University of California Chronicle*, vol. 10, no. 4 (May 4, 1908), https://sites.google.com/site/thorsteinveblenmurillocruzdsc/artigos-selecionados-de-veblen/evolution (accessed online 29 March 2011).
[4] Figures provided by Major Robert W. Erdman, U.S. Army G1 (Director, Personnel Strength and Analysis Forecasting) to the Author, 9 March 2011; information in author's possession.

sustainment force that will be unable, or simply unwilling, to answer the call when the first blasts of the next conflict sound.

Relevance

A study of recent campaigns will demonstrate that an over-reliance upon contracted logistics capacity has left the U.S. without a viable logistics Theater Opening Force able to conduct an operation on a Desert Storm level, or even to a level similar to the early, non-permissive phases of Operation Iraqi Freedom. Although many civilian logistics contractors are willing and able to operate in certain types of conflicts, most are ill suited to operate in a theater opening role or provide sustainment to U.S. military forces in a large scale protracted conflict. This reliance upon civilian contractors will severely limit America's ability to conduct large-scale military operations in an increasingly unpredictable and dangerous world. Just as the military has a propensity to fight the current war using the tactics of the last war regardless of the existing tactical or political situation, the U.S. military has fallen into the same trap concerning logistics support to its ground forces. In an effort to maximize efficiencies, the Department of Defense has increased its reliance upon a contracted logistics force structure, replacing many functions that would have been the mission of military logistics units with a contracted effort. However, the commercial corporations charged with logistics support at the tactical and operational levels may not be available or willing to participate in the next initial entry scenario regardless of the cash thrown at them. The number of maneuver "tooth" units within the American ground military simply does not matter if contracted logisticians are not capable—or simply not willing—to sustain them in the tactical and operational environment. Consequently, if not remedied, this reliance upon a

4

civilian/contracted military logistics capability to support our ground maneuver units at the tactical and operational levels of war will limit America's future war fighting capability and undermine any guarantee of U.S. security.

Methodology

To create a common frame of reference, this paper begins with a discussion of the type of warfare the U.S. military expects to face in the future. American combat in the environment of high intensity conflict (HIC), counter-insurgency (COIN) and hybrid warfare requires different logistics capabilities. Indeed, one size does not fit all.[5] As a point of comparison, in Chapter Two this paper reviews Desert Storm from the perspective of logistics. The intent is not to date the product or give a history lesson on the genesis of Desert Storm, but rather discuss the initial entry logistics and sustainment requirements for a military theater opening force in excess of 500,000 military servicemen and women. This chapter also reviews the post-Desert Storm force structure cuts, concentrating not only on the number of units cut, but specifically the type of units eliminated, ending with a review of our current logistics force structure and capability. Additionally, to investigate the hypothesis of a logistics capability gap, this paper uses products from the Joint Center for Operational Analysis (JCOA) concerning the type of wars/conflicts the United States may become involved with in the future. Chapters Three

---

[5] Emerging joint doctrine only lists two broad categories of war—traditional warfare and irregular warfare. According to Joint Publication 1 (draft), *traditional warfare* is characterized as a violent struggle for domination between nations or coalitions and alliances of nation-states, and is labeled "traditional" because it has been the pre-eminent form of warfare in the West since the Peace of Westphalia in 1648 dictated that nation-states alone have a monopoly on the legitimate use of force. The same document defines *irregular warfare* as characterized by a violent struggle among state and non-state actors for legitimacy and influence over relevant populations. The author of this thesis defined the types of warfare using their "historical" connotation of high intensity conflict (HIC), counter-insurgency (COIN) and hybrid (a mixture of traditional and irregular warfare), considering that Joint Publication 1 is in draft form only and not yet a Chairman of the Joint Chiefs of Staff approved document. U.S. Department of Defense. *Joint Publication 1: Doctrine for the Armed Forces of the United States (Revision First Draft),* (Washington, D.C., Government Printing Office, December 2010), 7-8.

and Four discuss two closely related topics. Chapter Three examines how the military establishment arrived at this predicament. Chapter Four offers a recommendation on how to correct this capability gap. Specifically, Chapter Three reviews logistics force ratios from World War II, the Korean Conflict, and the Vietnam War, comparing them to current logistics force ratios and offering thoughts on why the Department of Defense has grown to rely upon logistics contractors on the battlefield. Recommendations for a way forward are in Chapter Four, with focus upon increasing military logistics capability and leveraging emerging logistics force structure, while arguing that there is still a necessary role for logistics contractors.

Finally, the intent of this research is to provide a framework for strategic planners to consider a "way ahead" with respect to America's future logistics/sustainment force structure and determine to what degree commercial contractors should exist in that force structure. However, this thesis is not all-inclusive. The scope of this document does not allow for a discussion of budgetary issues in detail, nor does the document cover exactly what changes each service should make regarding specific military occupational specialties (MOSs) or equipment that must be procured to correct the sustainment capability differential. Force planners will have to conduct additional research to reach these conclusions. Nonetheless, this thesis will provide a starting point for critical thinkers to adjust U.S. logistics force structure to ensure the national command authority has the strategic flexibility to employ military forces when and where necessary.

CHAPTER 1: WARFARE DEFINED

"Amateurs study strategy, professionals study logistics." This quote, attributed to the 27th Commandant of the Marine Corps, General Robert H. Barrow, is not intended to belittle strategists, but rather accentuate the importance of logistics (and sustainment, before the term became popular) to military planners. Logistics is the cornerstone of success on the battlefield. From August through November 1944, General Patton's Third Army was resupplied via "Red Ball Express"—massive convoys of supplies pushed directly from the newly captured beach ports along the French coast—during its pursuit of German forces across France, Belgium and Germany. Without this sustainment action, Patton's Forces would have been left without the fuel, ammunition, or food required to carry on the fight.[1] This massive sustainment effort was critical to the success of Patton's Third Army as well as the defeat of German Forces.

Conversely, in an ironically similar situation over a year earlier, logisticians in Rommel's Afrika Korps miscalculated the amount of supplies called for by Rommel's Northern African Campaign plan. However, unlike the Third Army a year later, the Germans were unable to recover. By the time they corrected their mistake, the Allies

---

[1] As history tells us, logisticians "saved the day" with the Red Ball Express. However, to be academically honest, logisticians were also the cause of the Third Army's sustainment predicament. Despite certain Hollywood accounts of GEN Patton being initially denied the fuel and ammunition to carry the fight to the Germans in lieu of Field Marshall Sir Bernard Montgomery's British forces, the fact was that Patton's logisticians—at least as far down as the Division level—grossly underestimated the logistics required (particularly fuel) given the rate of advance Patton called for in his pursuit plan, as well as the high probability of enemy contact. The Third Army pursuit began 1 August 1944, and all subordinate divisions were all but out of fuel by 7 August 1944. One division—the 6th Armored--used almost three times the amount initially estimated. Patton's logisticians initially failed him, with what could have been catastrophic results. It is ironic that a similar situation hastened the demise of Rommel's Afrika Corps slightly over a year earlier, and truly ironic that Rommel made the statement referenced in footnote 2 of this chapter. Also, *Operation Barbarossa*—the Invasion of Russia—logistically fared no better for the Wehrmacht. The sustainment capability needed never materialized throughout the operation, primarily due to a lack of transportation capacity combined with poor transportation planning for the assets they did have, as opposed to a lack of supplies, that once again hastened the demise of several German Armies. The Army in World War Two. "The Red Ball Express." The JCS Group, http://www.jcs-group.com/military/war1941army/etoredball.html (accessed online 13 December 2010).

thwarted German strategic level sustainment efforts. British, then later American, forces interdicted resupply by sea, attacked ports, and destroyed German aircraft and ground convoys that attempted to transport the minimal amount of supplies available for German Forces. Though certainly not the single point of failure for the German North African Campaign, Rommel's logistics shortages were a significant factor is the Afrika Korps' surrender in May of 1943. Almost prophetically, Erwin Rommel stated in 1937 that, "In a man-to-man fight, the winner is he who has one more round in his magazine."[2] There has never been a more true statement. A military that is more tactically proficient than its foe will not be victorious if it does not have the materiel to complete the task.

Setting the Scene

One must clarify two key issues before embarking on a discussion of logistics and sustainment. First, although often used interchangeably, *logistics* and *sustainment* have distinctly different meanings. According to Joint Publication (JP) 3-0, *logistics* is the "science of planning, preparing, executing, and assessing the movement and maintenance of forces."[3] Logistics encompasses the integration of support efforts at the tactical, operational, and strategic levels of warfare, to include the mobilization and deployment of units. Supply, maintenance, transportation, health service support, explosive ordnance disposal, field services, and general engineering are areas of expertise typically categorized under the logistics banner.[4] JP 3-0 defines *sustainment* as "the provision of logistics and personnel services necessary to maintain and prolong operations until

---

[2] Erwin Johannes Eugen Rommel, *Infanterie greift an (Infantry Attacks,* 1937), 60.
[3] U.S. Department of Defense. *Joint Publication 3-0: Joint Operations,* (Washington, D.C., Government Printing Office, March 2010), III-30.
[4] Ibid.

mission accomplishment."[5] Simply put, sustainment gives the supported unit the items and services it needs to conduct its mission. It enables the supported unit the freedom of action and endurance to conduct operations, to include coordinating all classes of supply, maintaining equipment, organizing field services, coordinating personnel support, maintaining infrastructure and doing almost anything else that does not fall into another joint function. To summarize the relationship between logistics and sustainment, logistics is a subset of sustainment.

Second, not all warfare is created equal. This chapter analyses three distinct types of warfare (conflict): *High Intensity Conflict, Counter Insurgency Warfare, and Hybrid Warfare.* A brief explanation of the characteristics of each will follow in subsequent paragraphs. In general, warfare is the method used in armed conflict against an enemy; it is "the how" of waging war. Understanding that the conduct of warfare differs is critical to understanding the context of how each type of war is fought. An accurate contextual understanding of the type of military action is essential, as that understanding helps combatants make correct force structure and force preparation choices as well as decide they should engage in kinetic and/or non-kinetic operations.[6] Likewise, one must also realize that the logistics forces and concepts of sustainment required to support the combat elements engaged in warfare differ just as distinctly as the forces do depending upon the type and duration of conflict.

Finally, logisticians must remain flexible and not necessarily wedded to a particular type of warfare, thus avoiding convincing themselves that the United States will "never fight *that* kind of war." Loss of sustainment flexibility on the battlefield

---

[5] *Joint Publication 3-0,* III-30.
[6] U.S. Department of Defense. *Joint Publication 1: Doctrine for the Armed Forces of the United States (Revision First Draft),* (Washington, D.C., Government Printing Office, December 2010), 7.

results in the loss of strategic, operational, and tactical flexibility for the maneuver commander, which ultimately means a high likelihood of failure at the tactical, theater and possibly national level against an adaptable enemy.

High Intensity Conflict

High Intensity Conflict (HIC) is a conflict between at least two nations or groups of nations using conventional military weapons and tactics, with success (victory) defined as the defeat of an adversary's armed forces, the destruction of an adversary's ability to wage war, and/or the seizure or retention of territory. World War I, World War II, and Korea are typical examples of high intensity conflicts. HIC typically assumes that the vast majority of the belligerents within a given region wear uniforms, with enemy insurgent forces playing a diminished role. Thus, any non-uniformed indigenous personnel are assumed non-belligerent and accepting of whatever outcome the belligerent governments impose, arbitrate, or negotiate. Additionally, this type of conflict has historically involved all domains of the battlespace--land, sea, and air--and now includes space and cyberspace warfare as well. For the logistician, supporting a high intensity conflict is exceedingly labor intensive in terms of the manpower and equipment required to move the vast amount of supplies necessary to support such a large operation. For example, in preparation for and during the execution of Operation Desert Storm (August 1990-August 1991), United States military logisticians drove over 51 million miles; pumped 1.3 billion gallons of petroleum products (roughly seven times the fuel consumption of all of the vehicles in Washington D.C. during the same time period); and delivered from the United States to units in Saudi Arabia and Kuwait approximately

10

33,100 containers (ranging 188 miles if placed end-to-end).[7] From a logistics and sustainment perspective, HIC is easily the most resource intensive way to fight a war!

Nonetheless, not all wars the United States has been, or will be, involved in are categorized as "high intensity conflicts." For the past ten years, the United States has been engaged in a counter-insurgency (COIN) conflict in Iraq and Afghanistan and with special operating forces in other parts of the globe such as Somalia and Yemen. Also, the American military's recent (with *recent* defined as within the last 60 years) combat experience has been overwhelmingly comprised of counter insurgency warfare, or conflicts with a significant counter-insurgency flavor. Of the eight conflicts fought prior to 11 September 2001, six have been purely regional—or smaller—conflicts or COIN fights (Bosnia, Serbia, Kosovo, Somalia, Panama, and Grenada). The Vietnam War was what is now known as a "hybrid conflict" and Desert Storm—the 100 hour war (with a six-month prelude)—was fought as a high intensity conflict, but was of short duration and simply never fully materialized as a HIC fight.

Counter-Insurgency (COIN) Warfare

Any discussion of counter-insurgency warfare must first begin by defining the term "insurgency." As defined in JP 1-02, an insurgency is "the organized use of subversion and violence by a group or movement that seeks to overthrow or force change of a governing authority. Insurgency can also refer to the group itself."[8] An insurgent group will attempt to exhaust the will of its opponent by waging a protracted conflict. Additionally, to be successful an insurgent force must have control over, and ultimately

---

[7] William G. Pagonis, *Moving Mountains-Lessons in Logistics and Leadership from the Gulf War,* (Boston: Harvard Business School Press, 1992), 1, 6.

[8] U.S. Department of Defense. *Joint Publication 1-02: Department of Defense Dictionary of Military and Associated Terms,* (Washington, D.C., Government Printing Office, December 2010), 184.

the support of, a given population. Conversely, success (victory) in *counter-insurgency (COIN)* occurs when the governing authority has gained or maintained control or influence over, as well as garnered the support of, the same particular relevant population.[9] As with an insurgency, the population defines success in a counter-insurgency. Modern day examples of insurgencies are easy to observe in the operations of Islamic extremists in Iraq and Afghanistan. All insurgencies are different, but they all share similar *asymmetric warfare* qualities in which insurgents use military and non-military tactics to exploit the weaker elements of a standing government or their security forces, or to simply offset the latter's expected superior quality or quantity. In a high intensity conflict, the goal is to capture terrain and/or defeat a standing military force. In an insurgency, insurgents attempt to influence a "target" population through blackmail, extortion, or simply promises of a better way of life. Moreover, there are no traditional "battle lines" in insurgency warfare. There is no secure rear area—the battlefield is fluid. Consequently, *counter-insurgency (COIN) warfare* is the use of civil engagements and military asymmetric warfare tactics to counter an enemy's insurgent operations. As witnessed in Iraq since 2006, counter-insurgency tactics require the use of several smaller bases (such as patrol bases and forward operating bases) closer to the population both sides seek to influence. Logistics operations in COIN warfare are easier to support simply because the smaller number of forces generally used in counter-insurgency operations require less overall support; distribution rather than volume becomes the challenge. Nonetheless, logisticians must still move millions of gallons of fuel as well as tons of supplies and equipment thousands of miles to support this type of conflict. However, compared to the mountain of material required of a High Intensity Conflict

---

[9] *Joint Publication 1*, 9.

12

environment, the logistics/sustainment effort required of a COIN fight is a mere foothill. This reduced logistics requirement is also a dual-edged sword, as the only points that insurgents will attempt to exploit are generally weaker, under protected combat logistics patrols (e.g.: logistics convoys). Given the non-contiguous nature of COIN operations— and as witnessed in Operations Iraqi and Enduring Freedom—Soldiers and Marines with logistics military occupational specialties (MOSs) face direct contact situations with the enemy similar to those faced by their brethren in traditional combat specialties.

Besides their typical tactics, some non-state groups have evolved their "steady-state" insurgency or unconventional operations to include tactics, techniques, and procedures normally associated with uniformed armies. Groups such as Hezbollah, the Taliban, and many elements of al Qaeda have acquired weapons and perfected tactics normally associated with nation-states, creating a hybrid type of warfare that blends the most dangerous portions of both unconventional warfare and high intensity conflict.

Hybrid Warfare

Hybrid warfare is essentially what the name implies--a combination of high intensity conflict and insurgent operations. In hybrid warfare, terrorist cells, insurgent groups, and other "non state" actors acquire and use technologically advanced weapons of increased lethality and overall sophistication. As described by security scholar Frank Hoffman, hybrid scenarios combine the lethality of nation-on-nation conflict with the protracted fervor of irregular warfare.[10] More ominously, United States Secretary of

---

[10] Frank G. Hoffman, "Hybrid Warfare, and Challenges." *Joint Forces Quarterly* (October 2009), 38.

Defense Robert Gates defines hybrid warfare as the place where "…Microsoft coexists with machetes…."[11]

The terrorist group Hezbollah offered a perfect example of hybrid warfare in action during its 2006 conflict with Israel. Hezbollah had a huge arsenal of rockets and mortars as well as much more advanced guided anti-ship missiles, rivaling the deadly army inventories of many nations. However, Hezbollah also continued to use its terrorist-style hit and run tactics as well as the use of suicide bombers to strike specific Israeli settlements on the West Bank and popular gathering spots in Tel Aviv and Jerusalem. Hezbollah mastered the soft and hard power mix necessary of hybrid warfare. It retained its ideological social service programs, generating the support of the Lebanese populace, while simultaneously employing increased firepower through the use of rockets, mortars and a few guided missiles. In July and August of 2006, Hezbollah struck Israel with an aggressiveness and destructive power previously unseen in the conflict. In about a 37 day period, besides the typical insurgent "hit and run" tactics, and command or victim operated IEDs, they attacked Israel with approximately 4,000 rockets, destroying almost 2,000 homes, killing more than 50 Israeli citizens, and injuring several thousand, along with causing the evacuation of an estimated 200,000 civilians. The same rocket attacks shut down Israel's major seaport—Haifa—as well as an associated refinery.[12] Hezbollah also launched four unmanned aerial vehicles (UAVs) against

---

[11] Robert M. Gates, "A Balanced Strategy: Reprogramming the Pentagon for a New Age." *Foreign Affairs,* 31.

[12] Uzi Rubin, *The Rocket Campaign Against Israel During the 2006 Lebanon War* (Ramat Gan, Israel: Began-Sadat Center for Strategic Studies, 2007), 10-14.

14

Israeli targets and sunk an Israeli Navy Corvette (coastal/littoral patrol boat) with a

Chinese built and Iranian-supplied Silkworm anti-ship guided missile.[13]

Hezbollah's use of nation-state firepower is simply an example. Non-state groups

can purchase virtually any weapon their fiscal resources might allow and that they can

import, as is clearly evidenced by Hezbollah's use of Chinese-made Silkworm missiles.

Hezbollah is certainly not the only non-state actor to have access to weapons more

typically associated with legitimate militaries. Al Qaeda-Iraq, the Taliban, and the

Chechen Rebels all use weapons and equipment associated with their respective

country's former Soviet compatriots/masters. Mortars, single and quad-mounted 12.7mm

DShK (Russian heavy machine guns), and in the case of the Taliban, T-55 tanks captured

from Afghanistan's former Northern Alliance, are common among their forces. The

complexity of a hybrid fight requires that military and civilian leaders and planners

develop innovative methods for fighting an enemy with very flexible and innovative

tactics. Using competitive fighting as a metaphor, fighting a true hybrid enemy is

somewhat akin to a pure boxer battling a mixed martial artist that is equally versed in

striking (Karate) and submission holds (Brazilian Jiu Jitsu). From a logistics standpoint,

the supported forces may not be as large as those during a high intensity conflict, but they

could be significantly larger than those supporting a strictly COIN fight. Additionally,

the enemy will continue to use the tactic of attacking targets perceived as weak or poorly

defended. Given their lack of heavily armored vehicles such as Abrams Tanks Bradley

Infantry Fighting Vehicles, logistics units—particularly convoys of thin-skinned fuel

trucks—will continue to make inviting, lucrative, and comparatively soft targets for

enemy forces.

---

[13] Andrew F. Krepinevich, *7 Deadly Scenarios* (New York: Bantam Books, 2009), 130.

Each type of warfare—high intensity conflict, counter-insurgency, and hybrid—has its own strategic differences, and each is used to fight a specific type of enemy using specific tactics. Similarly, each type of warfare has its own unique logistics force requirements. In light of Clausewitz's admonition to "understand the nature of the war upon which you are about to enter," it is prudent to discuss the sort of war the U.S. will need to prepare for in the future.[14]

The Threat

People only see what they are prepared to see.[15]
  -Ralph Waldo Emerson

Early on a Sunday morning on the seventh of the month, a combatant fleet approached the Hawaiian Islands. It continued to steam eastward at high speed toward the island chain, but stayed well north of the normal shipping lanes. The fleet's commander had ordered strict radio silence and light discipline, as the success of their operation depended upon stealth and the element of surprise. At approximately 100 nautical miles from their primary objective—Pearl Harbor—the fleet turned into the prevailing wind and launched their attack aircraft in the pre-dawn darkness. A mixture of fighters, dive bombers, and torpedo planes, the invaders sped toward their respective objectives unnoticed. Just as dawn broke, the dive bombers and torpedo bombers attacked the United States Navy's battleships, cruisers, destroyers and the occasional supply ship at anchor at Pearl Harbor, while the fighters strafed aircraft sitting neatly on the ground at nearby Hickam Field. Virtually all of the Navy's ships at anchor were struck at least once. By the time the Army Air Corps (AAC) pilots were able to man the

---

[14] Carl von Clausewitz, *On War,* ed. and trans. Michael Howard and Peter Paret (New York: Alfred A. Knopf, 1976), 100.
[15] Emerson as quoted in Krepinevich, 1.

undamaged planes at Hickam, the attacking aircraft had gone, only to reappear for a second wave attack after the AAC pilots had landed to refuel. The surprise attack was an overwhelming success for the attacking force and an utter disaster for the Navy and Army Air Corps in and around Pearl Harbor.

The date was 7 January 1932 and the action was a joint U.S. Army-Navy wargame called Grand Joint Exercise 4.[16] The torpedoes dropped had no warheads and the "bombs" were bags of flour that merely dusted the decks of ships at anchor. Nonetheless, the Army, embarrassed by such an attack, cried foul, claiming that the attacking carriers had been sighted and previously attacked, and that it was unlikely that any potential adversary would commence an attack on a Sunday morning. Exercise umpires agreed, saying that it was "...doubtful that air attacks could be launched against Oahu in the face of strong defensive aviation without subjecting the attacking carriers to material damage and subsequent great loss...."[17]

The actual Japanese attack on Pearl Harbor not ten years later was just as effective in surprising U.S. forces as the previous wargame—only this time with more devastating and deadly consequences. As America advances into the middle of the twenty-first century, senior defense officials and military leaders must avoid another such strategic and operational surprise and resist easy and false conclusions about the emerging state of warfare by ignoring, dismissing as irrelevant, or simply being wrong about any potential future threats. Looking into the future, it is difficult to pinpoint the most dangerous threat faced by the United States with absolute certainty. History has proven humans highly inadequate when it comes to the task of predicting the future of warfare. As

---

[16] Krepinevich., 1-4.
[17] Ibid., 4.

argued by Michael C. Horowitz and Dan A. Shalon in "The Future of War and American Military Strategy," "Empirically, the next war is rarely like the preceding one—especially when comparing larger conflicts."[18] For example, a theoretical analyst attempting to predict the future security environment 20 years hence, beginning in 1900 and continuing every decade (1900-1920; 1910-1930; 1920-1940;…2000-2020; 2010-2030) would have achieved little success. As an example using the same timeline, a "futurist" would have missed both World War I and World War II, possibly not predicted Hitler's invasion of his neighbors or Japan's attack on Pearl Harbor, or the rise of the Cold War between the United States and the Soviet Union. Continuing on this linear progression, a prediction in 1980 would have missed the end of the Cold War and a 1990 prediction would have missed attacks of 11 September 2001.[19] Regardless of the systematic prediction model used, this example shows that the future is inherently non-linear and incredibly difficult to predict with accuracy.

As the eminent British military historian Sir Michael Howard suggests, the best a military organization can hope for when attempting to predict its future defense requirements is to "not get it too badly wrong."[20] In these days of a dwindling defense budgets, DoD must spend every dollar well. The programming and budgeting process does not happen overnight; resourcing manpower and equipment for a particular "fight" takes a decade or more. After a decade of war, the United States is just now becoming adept at a combined, whole of government approach to counter insurgency. This flash-to-bang time concerning what the next war will be--"nextwaritis" as strategists Horowitz

---

[18] Michael A. Horowitz and Dan A. Shalon, "The Future of War and American Military Strategy." Orbis (Spring 2009), 308.

[19] Ibid., 308-309.

[20] Michael Howard, "Military Science in an Age of Peace," *RUSI: The Journal of the Royal United Services Institute,* 119 (March 1974), 7.

and Shalon have dubbed it--is a critical factor in why planners must be as accurate as possible in their predictions.[21] For in a globalized, interconnected world, the United States will not have time to fix mistakes in planning by re-tooling its factories or adding more training capacity as it has in the past. While the future may be unpredictable, the rapidity of change and the interdependence of world systems mandates the U.S. military be in a constant state of readiness.

There are those who will argue that the United States is destined to fight only smaller, regional conflicts or counter-insurgencies in the future. Andrew F. Krepinevich, President of the Center of Strategic and Budgetary Assessments, argues that the most likely future conflicts will be irregular and the United States military should prepare accordingly.[22] He is not alone. Thomas X. Hammes, retired Marine Colonel and COIN expert, as well as Army Brigadier General H.R. McMaster argue that the United States military relies on a "functionally flawed conception of future war" and should abandon "wrongheaded thinking," placing more effort into correcting the force structure required for the COIN fights that are sure to come.[23] John Nagl, a retired Army lieutenant colonel and a member of the team that wrote FM 3-24, the joint Army/Marine Counter-Insurgency manual, also states "…COIN will continue to be the face of battle in the 21st century."[24] This same group also believes that contractors adequately support our deployed military forces and are a "safe bet" considering their belief that a larger conflict is not forthcoming. Nonetheless, recent events indicate that, while the United States

[21]Horowitz and Shalon, 301.

[22] Andrew Krepinevich, "The Future of U.S. Ground Forces: Challenges and Requirements," 17 April 2007, http://www.csbaonline.org/4Publications/PubLibrary/T.20070417.The_Future_of_US_G/T.20070417.The_Future_of_US_G.pdf (accessed 19 February 2011), 12-13.

[23] Horowitz and Shalon, 303-304.

[24] John Nagl, "Institutionalizing Adaption: It's Time for a Permanent Army Advisor Corps," http://www.cnas.org/files/documents/.../Nagl_AdvisoryCorp_June07.pdf (accessed 20 January 2010).

military must be ready to execute any type of contingency operation, there remains a significant threat of a high intensity conflict or a hybrid conflict with a significant nation-state influence.

With its military-related technological advances of the past two decades, China is a favorite potential HIC threat of some students of political-military strategy. China's "red line"—the line that must be crossed for its leadership to commit to direct military action—has five potential "go to war" scenarios, four of which relate directly to Taiwan.[25]

1) A Taiwanese declaration of independence.
2) Taiwan seeking nuclear weapons.
3) Military pact between Taiwan and the United States involving the staging of American Troops on Taiwanese soil.
4) If China must commit forces to Taiwan to "keep the peace" (e.g.: failure of Taiwan's Government).
5) Retaining freedom of movement in the Strait of Malacca for the Chinese Naval forces and Chinese related energy commerce.[26]

Regardless of the potential triggers, there is little likelihood of a direct conflict between the United States and the Peoples' Republic of China for several reasons. First, neither country is spoiling for a fight yet likes the benefits of having a major-power adversary to serve as a focal point for defense strategy and resourcing. For the United States, China provides the new "boogeyman" for political and popular attention, as the country withdraws from COIN fights in Iraq (2011) and Afghanistan (2014). Similarly for China, the United States represents a reason to evolve militarily, with the hope that economic power as well as academic and scientific advances will ride on the back of this

---

[25] David Winterford, A Clash of Civilizations: China. TH6116B Joint Advanced Warfighting School lecture, Norfolk, VA, 6 January 2011.

[26] Approximately 80% of China's imported oil comes through the Strait of Malacca, and they will fight to control it. According to a Chinese Naval strategist, "The Strait of Malacca is akin to breathing— like life itself." U.S. Joint Forces Command. *The Joint Operating Environment (JOE) 2010:* (Suffolk, VA: United States Joint Forces Command, February 18, 2010), 41.

military progression. The academic and technological rigor required to build a new Peoples' Liberation Army (PLA) is quite extensive, creating not only a technological renaissance, but a rebirth of critical thinking as well.[27] Chinese military schools at all levels have augmented their traditional Eastern philosophy of warfare with a study of Clausewitz and Jomini as well as a study of relatively recent history such as why communism failed in the former Soviet Union. Also, a China armed with a naval modernization program including at least one nuclear powered aircraft carrier and a fleet of ultra-quiet submarines will soon be capable of power projection on a scale rivaling that of the United States. This newly developed capability gives the Chinese hegemony over their "near-abroad" in a manner similar to that of Japan prior to World War II. That said, neither China nor the U.S. want to risk conflict over less than vital national interests. The economic costs and the devastation such a conflict would cause, particularly given the possibility of a nuclear conflict, far outweigh any potential tactical or political gain. Regarding any direct military confrontation, the American military is certainly a match for the Chinese in a *conventional* (e.g.: non-nuclear) confrontation, and would defeat them based upon the United States Navy's ability to control the Strait of Malacca—thus starving China of its oil imports—as well as American strategic bomber and tactical fighter quantitative and qualitative superiority. However, a high intensity conflict fight among the two military super powers has a likelihood of "going nuclear", with mutually assured destruction (MAD) becoming more than a pithy phrase. Both countries have an extensive nuclear capability with any potential nuclear conflict scenario not difficult to envision. An exchange of nuclear weapons would likely increase in severity as each country attempts to protect its own national interest. The Chinese, viewed by

---

[27] *Joint Operating Environment 2010,* 40.

"nextwaritis" HIC proponents as an aggressor, know that any nuclear conflict would be devastating to them as well. Their military, in addition to key pieces of their infrastructure, would be obliterated, thereby destroying any potential they have for gaining the political, military, and economic parity that they seek with the United States.

Second, America and China are economically interdependent. American and Chinese business ventures are becoming increasingly common—and lucrative—in the hosting country. Coca-Cola, Starbucks, Wynn Resorts, and Ford have invested hundreds of millions of dollars in China during recent years. Coca-Cola and Starbucks consider China to be their fastest growing market, while Wynn Resorts will open its second casino in Macau in June 2010, with plans for a third already approved. Not to be outdone, Las Vegas-Sands, Incorporated is scheduled to open the largest casino in the Macau area during the 1st Quarter 2012. Ford Motor Company is opening a $490 million plant at Chongqingin in late 2012 to produce the Ford Focus model vehicle for Chinese domestic consumption and possibly world-wide export. With Ford's Chinese domestic vehicles sales reaching approximately 153,000 during FY 2010—an increase of almost 84 percent over the same quarter of the previous fiscal year—company officials expect a continued increase in their Chinese market share. Potential sales in other areas of consumer goods make China a critical draw for other industries as well. With a growing middle class, Heinz Foods, Apple Computers, Nike, and The Gap have also begun to fight for their respective product market share within the country.[28]

---

[28] Epstein, Gady and Robyn Meredith. "US Companies that Invest Big in China: American Companies Invest in China, Chasing Global Growth," *Forbes.Com* (5 July 2010), www.forbes.com/2010/07/05/us-investments-china-markets-emerging-markets-fdi.html (accessed online 8 March 2011).

Conversely, China is investing in the United States on an even grander scale. As has been widely publicized, China owns approximately $894.8 billion in U.S. debt in the form of Treasury bills, but they have also invested almost an additional $500 billion in other ventures.[29] The Chinese have capitalized on a weak dollar, investing in the United States while asset prices were depressed. Chinese investments are varied, ranging from Solix Biofuels—a Colorado firm working to turn algae into a fuel source—to Hawaii based alternate energy company Hoku Scientific as well as auto parts manufacturer Delphi, Incorporated. The state owned holding company—China Investment Corporation—has also spent approximately $300 billion to invest in world-wide soft drink leader Coca-Cola and well known financial entities such as Morgan-Stanley and equity giant, The Blackstone Group. The Chinese have taken advantage of a less-than-stellar American real estate market, spending several hundred million dollars in real estate related funds managed by the Goldman-Sachs Group and Oaktree Capital of Los Angeles.[30] In sum, the United States based companies have invested approximately $600 billion in China, while the Chinese have invested, by many accounts, as much as $1.3 trillion in the United States. Neither nation wants to risk their investment with an overt act of war.

Lastly, war with China is highly unlikely because America will continue to walk a fine strategic line in their relationship with China and Taiwan, particularly given the shared historical differences between the two nations. As stated previously, four of the

---

[29] Reuters. "Chinese Investment in the U.S.: $2 Trillion and Counting," http://blogs.reuters.com/india-expertzone/2011/03/02/chinese-investment-in-us-2-trln-and-counting/ (accessed 9 March 2011).
[30] Lee, Don. "China Investments in the U.S. Up Sharply", *LA Times Online,* 4 March 2010 http://articles.latimes.com/2010/mar/04/business/la-fi-china-invest4-2010mar04 (accessed 9 March 2011).

five reasons that China might go to war with the United States center upon Taiwan, with the United States being the pivot point for any potential conflict. The "fine line" the U.S. will walk is *strategic ambiguity,* through which the United States will seek to avoid a confrontation with China over Taiwan, while retaining the strategic basing required of U.S. Navy assets. Through strategic ambiguity, America never agrees explicitly to a Taiwanese request to defend Taiwan against China, but also never tells China that Taiwan will not be defended.[31]

Regardless of its increasing military prowess, it is simply not in China's strategic interest to go to war with the United States. A desire for a strong economy and to be a world leader drive China's actions. However, the fact remains that China has emerged as a peer/military competitor to the United States, and it is prudent for the U.S. to take China's *capabilities* into consideration. The possibility of conflict exists, but the likelihood is low.

Some consider Russia in the same vein, with a worse-case scenario being a hybrid war that includes the use of a weapon of mass destruction and ultimately, U.S. military involvement.[32] Fortunately, potential "issues" with Russia are now largely regional as opposed to global and primarily concerning the nation-states of the former Soviet Union and a healthy Russian fear of China as well. Thus, the likelihood of a direct conflict with the United States within the next ten years is slim. However, the U.S. may have to deal with the consequences of a conflict between Russia and at least one of its former satellites or a possible dispute with China concerning Chinese immigration into Russian Eastern territories.

---

[31] David Winterford.

[32] Olga Oliker and Tanya Charlik-Paley, *Assessing Russia's Decline—Trends and Implications for the United States and the U.S. Air Force* (Santa Monica, CA: Rand Corporation, 2002), 98-109.

Called by Vladimir Putin "the greatest geopolitical catastrophe of the century," the 1990 disintegration of the Soviet Union was only the beginning of a tumultuous future for the region.[33] With the collapse of the Soviet Union, the majority of the territories controlled, or at least significantly influenced, by Russia for the last 100 years went their separate ways. The collapse not only destroyed the Soviet economic structure—as anemic as it was in many respects—but also brought into power a weak democratic government incapable of controlling the criminal enterprises that were gaining influence within the country, nor able to establish a legitimate economy.

Upon succeeding Boris Yeltsin as President of the Russian Federation, Vladimir Putin began instituting policy changes to create a strong central government and reinforce the economy. Using an influx of foreign cash produced by its oil refining and natural gas production industry, Russia has been able to emerge from the economic low-point of the early 1990s.[34] However, Russia did not use the income produced through the sale of their petroleum products to improve antiquated oil facilities, but rather to bolster Russian military buildup.[35] Between 2001 and 2006, the Russian Government has quadrupled their military budget with increases over 20% per year. Also, in 2007 the Russian Parliament voted to approve sizably larger defense appropriations through 2015.[36] The Russian end state does not appear designed to create the military monster reminiscent of the former Soviet Union, but rather to retain the ability to influence its former satellite states, have military credibility with the West and with China, and further its regional interests.

---

[33] *Joint Operating Environment 2010,* 42.
[34] Ibid., 42-43.
[35] Keith Dickson. A Clash of Civilizations: Russia. TH 6116A (Joint Advanced Warfighting School lecture, Norfolk, VA, January 5, 2011).
[36] *Joint Operating Environment 2010,* 44.

Given its relatively recent history with Chechnya as well as terrorism in the Caucasus, and a Central Asia with unstable, newly "created" oil-rich nations along with a 4300 mile recently demarcated border with China, Russia's security plate is full. Nonetheless, Russia feels it must be able to control the region, as opposed to establishing methods of peacefully working with its neighbors for the good of all concerned. The common theme across the region is one of Russian meddling. As stated in the Joint Forces Command's 2010 Joint Operating Environment (JOE), Russia is playing a much "more active but less constructive role in the region." Through Russia's direct support to separatists in parts of Georgia as well as indirect support in the Armenian and Azerbaijani conflict, these regional fights are guaranteed to continue. To Russian delight, these governments spends their resources on fighting what are effectively civil wars, further impoverishing the people and leading to organized crime, lawlessness, and an all but total disregard for legitimate authority instead of creating stable, prosperous democracies.[37]

Consequently, Russia faces an uncertain future concerning its relationship in the region. Russia's problem can be surmised as having to hold on to a geographically large, populous, economically, ethnically and politically diverse geography without using force.[38] However, operating "without force" is simply not in Russia's nature; Russia wants to be seen as an equal to the United States and China and views the calculated use of force as a means to that end. Although not the old "Soviet Bear", the Russians believe that directly involving themselves into regional nation-state internal conflicts will likely give them the credibility they seek. Russia will likely use its renewed military capability

---

[37] *Joint Operating Environment 2010*, 42-44.
[38] Keith Dickson. A Clash of Civilizations: Russia. TH 6116A (Joint Advanced Warfighting School lecture, Norfolk, VA, January 5, 2011).

to regain control—albeit not legitimate governmental control—of its former provinces in the name of safeguarding Russian nationals in border regions.[39] Russian military force against its neighbors is where the possibility of conflict exists between the United States and Russia. U.S. intervention in any Russian attempt of direct action against one of its smaller neighbors would almost certainly result in conflict between the two nations.

Of primary concern to the United States is the safeguarding of former Soviet nuclear, biological, and chemical warheads and material. The security of weapons of mass destruction (WMD) as well as the non-proliferation of nuclear weapons capability (e.g.: fissile material, weapon components, as well as completed weapons) to other nations, and particularly to terrorist groups, continues to be an objective of the United States. Of equal concern, particularly in Europe, is Russia's use of oil and gas supplies as a lever to pry political concessions from its neighbors. Europe relies heavily upon natural gas from Russian and her neighboring states.[40] Not only does Russia conveniently threaten to reduce the flow of gas to the south, but it essentially has a corner on the natural gas market, with little competition from the antiquated, Soviet era gas production facilities in the smaller, former Soviet satellite countries. Any Russian aggression against her neighbors would potentially place control of all of the region's natural gas in Russian hands, not a condition for which Europe is prepared, but one which it may have to respond. Consequently, as long as weapons of mass destruction are

---

[39] Russia plays on ethnic and national tensions if it serves their purpose. In this case, Russia may take direct action (attack) its neighbors under the guise of "freeing" the minority Russian citizens in a given border region. U.S. Joint Forces Command. *The Joint Operating Environment 2010*, 41-44.

[40] According to the 5 January 2007 report by the Congressional Research Service, "Russian Natural Gas: Regional Dependence" (http://www.fas.org/sgp/crs/misc/RS22562.pdf), accessed 10 March 2011, as an example 39% of German, 69% of Austrian, and 82% of Greek natural gas consumed is supplied by Russia.

safeguarded and the gas continues to flow, the U.S. and its allies will not become involved in "disagreements" between the former Soviet Union and its satellite states.

As recent events in Libya demonstrate, China and Russia are certainly not the only possibilities for future conflict. As nation-state failures and the possibility of government radicalization continues, hybrid threats will be of significant concern in the future. Hybrid conflicts can erupt anywhere there is state failure, a non-state group to fill the power void, and typical uniformed military type equipment and a personnel organization. Given a structured enemy currently practicing unconventional warfare with access to weapons typically associated with a uniformed nation-state military, the linkages between high intensity conflict warfare and irregular/insurgency warfare are much more likely than many believe. These future hybrid wars will be comprised of interlocking elements of war, some more conventional in nature, and others largely irregular.[41] The overthrow of Egypt's Hosni Mubarak in February 2011 along with the current undeclared civil war in Libya—with its real potential for long-term U.S. involvement—will continue to have a destabilizing effect in the region and provides a perfect backdrop for this discussion.

In what has been dubbed the "Jasmine Revolution," the Tunisian Government under Ben Ali fell on 31 January 2011 in an action that ignited a wave of political instability across the region. Mubarak's fall in Egypt was soon to follow. Post Egypt, the current concern is an undeclared civil war in Libya with the possibility of long-term U.S. involvement. The concern now is "what's next"? According to strategist Kees Van der Heijden, "You must spend time hunting for surprises; otherwise, it is

[41] Michelle A. Flournoy and Shawn Brimely, "The Defense Inheritance: Challenges and Choices for the Next Pentagon Team," *The Washington Quarterly* (Autumn 2008), 64.

difficult not to come up with the obvious."[42] This advice, combined with Clausewitz's statement that "…surprise lies at the foundation of all undertakings…," cautions the U.S. Department of Defense to prepare for the next unknown, the next "what if" scenario.

Scenarios

Consequently, in preparing for the next conflict, planners must think beyond our current enemy and consider who a potential enemy may be and how they would likely fight. As discussed in the introduction of this thesis, prognostication for future conflicts is poor at best. The U.S. military has a propensity to plan for the last war instead of anticipating the next set of combat conditions. One way to avoid similar problems in the future is to use fact-based scenarios to force planners to think "outside of the box." If done properly, working through a potential military eventuality through the use of a scenario will help the DoD to prepare for the next conflict instead of refighting the last one.

Libya is a perfect country to use as a scenario example. Given the current situation in Libya, it is prudent for U.S. strategists to consider the possibilities of how the current crisis will run its course. The wild card in the Libyan civil war is the country's leader, Moammar Qaddafi. Certainly an eccentric individual, Qaddafi's past history of arguably paranoid schizophrenic behavior deserves consideration. With self-proclaimed monikers such as "The Mad Dog of the Middle East" and the "King of Kings", Qaddafi is a leader who would certainly stop at nothing to right a perceived wrong, such as a U.S. enforced no-fly-zone over Libya or other forms of severe sanctions.

---

[42] Kees Van der Heijden, *Scenarios: The Art of Strategic Communication* (Hoboken, New Jersey: John Wiley and Sons, 2005), 59.

Also, the so-named Libyan civil war is not only significant because of the instability it continues to brew in the region, but for the weapons that could fall into the hands of America's enemies—either used by the dictator himself, willfully given/sold by Qaddafi, or taken from a post-Qaddafi government by force. In addition to the relatively mundane—but all important to legitimate armies and terrorists world-wide—mortars, free-flying katusha-type rockets, AK-47s and Dragonov sniper rifles, the Libyan Army also has a plethora of SA-7s shoulder fired anti-aircraft missiles as well as SA-8a Gecko anti-aircraft systems (short range, single staged, multiple launch guided anti-aircraft missiles on a wheeled chassis). Additionally, Qaddafi's forces also have a suspected 11.75 tons of mustard gas, SCUD-B delivery systems, and unspecified amounts of "yellow cake" uranium that may be sold for raw cash.[43]

There are several possible branch scenarios given Libya's current realities, with three listed below. All have a common type-of-warfare theme.

First: ***U.S. enforced no-fly zone.*** The United States enforces a no-fly zone over Libya, effectively keeping the Libyan Air Force grounded and unable to conduct air-ground integration (AGI) operations with Libyan Government ground forces. The Libyan Rebel forces gain a foothold again, and Qaddafi and his military are once again on the run. Out of desperation, Qaddafi launches a mustard gas attack on his own civilian population at and behind Rebel lines, and threatens to do the same to any U.S. military forces in the area. Does the United States attack the Qaddafi's SCUD launch sites? If so—how? Will ground troops be introduced at the risk of being called another infidel

---

[43] Jay Solomon. "U.S. Fears Tripoli May Employ Gas as Chaos Mounts," *The Wall Street Journal,* 24 February 2011.

invasion and war for oil? What next? For an added twist, what if a U.S. aircraft gets shot down, even if there has been no previous direct contact with Libyan forces?

Second: ***U.S. enforced no-fly zone, version two.*** Just as in the scenario above, the United States enforces a no-fly zone over Libya, once again effectively curtailing Qaddafi's attacks on opposition forces. The current Libyan government is near defeat, but is joined in the fight against "the western invaders" by other Muslim extremist groups that have previously not been directly involved in the fight. In this scenario, groups such as al-Qaeda in the Islamic Mahgreb, al Shabaab, or the Taliban will have access to mustard gas, SCUD-Bs and a variety of other "nation-state" type weapons with which to fight against the United States. Once again---now what? In spite of Secretary Gates' warning that "…any future defense secretary that advises the President to send a big land army into Asia or into the Middle East should have his head examined…," does the U.S. place troops on the ground, or simply allow the Libyan Rebels—whom we have presumably pledged to help and given legitimacy to simply through our no-fly zone presence—as well as the civilians that support them, to be slaughtered by Qaddafi and his band of additional Muslim extremists?[44]

Last: ***Post Qaddafi Government unfriendly to the U.S.*** Despite U.S. support for a no-fly zone, victorious Libyan Rebels coalesce into a "new" Libyan Government that is unfriendly to the United States and is ideologically attached to and influenced by al Qaeda in the Islamic Mahgreb and al Shabaab. The American intelligence community is concerned that the new Libya will not only be an active supporter of state sponsored

---

[44] Thom Shanker. "Warning Against Wars Like Iraq and Afghanistan", *New York Times Online,* 25 February 2011 http://www.nytimes.com/2011/02/26/world/26gates.html (accessed 9 March 2011).

31

terrorism, but provide weapons—and potentially weapons of mass destruction—to the terrorists. How does the United States face this challenge? Does the United States use containment, similar to what has been done with Iran, or do we take a more active, direct stance considering Libya's open relationship with known terrorist organizations and the weapons they may provide to them? What's next?

The common denominator or common "type of war" theme in all of these scenarios is hybrid warfare. Whenever a terrorist group has access to weapons normally reserved for a typical uniformed nation-state military, hybrid warfare is a strong possibility. Any military forces placed on the ground in Libya will not only face typical terrorist type "hit and run" tactics, but they will face a force that has access to advanced weapons such as multiple launch rocket systems, anti-ship guided missiles, armored vehicles and aircraft. Much like the Hezbollah force the Israeli military faced in Lebanon in the late summer of 2006, a "hybrid enemy" fights insurgency warfare augmented by a significant conventional capability.

As the President of Egypt, Mubarak provided a stabilizing force in the region, an element in America's favor that may no longer exist. Certainly a friend, if not always a full supporter of the United States and the West in a largely anti-U.S./Western part of the globe, Mubarak's Egypt also sustained a peace treaty with Israel, much to the chagrin of many in the Arab world. In a recent interview concerning recent events in Egypt, former Secretary of State Henry Kissinger stated that a future Egypt has "…more pro-Islamic, anti-Israel, anti-U.S. forces than pure democrats the way we understand it."[45] There is

---

[45] Henry Kissinger, "The U.S. Should Be Careful in Egypt," 1 February 2011, http://www.newsmax.com/TheWire/Kissinger-U-SCareful-Egypt/2011/02/01/id/384589#ixzz1EWFU3Le2 (accessed 20 February 2011).

every reason to believe in the likelihood that any other country in the region—Libya,

Morocco, Yemen and Bahrain included—that is on the brink of so-called "democracy"

will emerge with an anti-Western political stance. Also, Iranian influence in the region

will continue to be a thorn in America's side, as radical Islamicism and a hatred for the

West will trump any potential Persian versus Arab differences. The Iranian Leadership

are seemingly always ready, willing and able to assist a new Islamic government in the

region, particularly if the new government replaces a previous government that was

friendly toward the United States. With the possibility of an anti-western influenced

"new" Egypt retaining control of the Suez Canal, the entire region is potentially

strategically vulnerable.

The "what if" factor of this entire chapter is that the United States military must

be prepared for whatever type of warfare emerges in the future. "Being prepared" not

only concerns just the maneuver (typical combat) forces, but the sustainers as well.

Military logisticians must know the kind of fight they will be expected to support and

how to support it. Given an analysis of America's potential enemies, current events in

the Middle East, the retrograde of ground forces from our current COIN operations in

Iraq and Afghanistan no later than 2014, and considering that it is not in China's strategic

interest to become involved in a direct conflict with the United States, a future hybrid war

is a very plausible scenario. The cornerstone of potential success is what the military

does with this strategic critical thinking. Leaders and strategists must not be satisfied

with the current plans on the shelf, or risk being surprised by an enemy action no one saw

coming. Plans are useless, but planning is indispensible, with planning for the

sustainment of U.S. forces key to combat success.

CHAPTER 2: SUSTAINMENT CAPABILITY—THEN VS. NOW

Bitter experience in war has taught the maxim that the art of war is the art of the logistically feasible.[1]
-ADM Hyman Rickover, USN

To say that logistics capability is a "force multiplier" would be akin to saying that Babe Ruth was a decent pinch hitter. Logistics capability—or more precisely said, sustainment capability—is critical to a nation's ability to wage war. Sustainment capability allows the force commander the freedom of action to plan and conduct maneuver warfare to defeat his enemies—regardless of the enemy tactical or operational scenario presented. This tactical and operational freedom of maneuver is the cornerstone of strategic flexibility, allowing the U.S. National Leadership to control the operational tempo of the conflict and fight our nation's enemies when, where and how we choose. Operation Desert Storm is a perfect example for studying the importance of raw logistics capacity and sustainment capability.

Operation Desert Storm

Aptly described by LTG(R) Gus Pagonis as a "logistical war in three phases— deployment, combat and redeployment," the logistics required and the sustainment plan developed and executed for Desert Storm was unprecedented in many respects.[2] As has been documented in this thesis, the "raw numbers" of material required—and supplied— was simply phenomenal. Within the first 90 days of the "deployment phase" (Operation Desert Shield), approximately 1.3 million tons of equipment and supplies were shipped and airlifted into theater; over 180,000 passengers were airlifted into theater (with a total supported population of over 560,000 by mid February 1991); an average of 35

---

[1] International Military Forums. "International Military Forum: About Logistics Quotes," found online at http://www.military-quotes.com/forum/logistics-quotes-t511.html (accessed 11 March 2011).
[2] Pagonis, 5.

commercial jetliners and/or military airlift aircraft along with 2.3 ships were received and off-loaded daily; and 12,435 tracked combat vehicles along with 117,157 wheeled vehicles received into country. These numbers are awe-inspiring for logisticians everywhere, but do not include other functions that made Desert Storm a success. Contracts for fuel, fresh food, billeting, and the upgrade of the base M1 Abrams tank to the M1A1 standard were all accomplished by uniformed service members and a handful of U.S. Government Service civilians.[3]

The redeployment of forces from Southwest Asia was just as impressive, and just as well executed. However, due to the compressed timeline to get American forces home as well as the retrograde of equipment and unused stockpiles of supplies, Operation Desert Farewell became a greater logistics challenge than Operation Desert Shield. Strategic planners believed that the United States (and their Coalition brethren) should expect ground combat operations to last approximately 30 days. Regardless of the 30-day estimation, Iraqi forces lost most of their will to fight after a five-week air campaign; the then estimated 30-day war turned into a 100-hour war in reality. Thus, Desert Farewell became a more daunting task than originally envisioned. The American political will driving the train to "get the Soldiers, Sailors, Airmen and Marines home," combined with the Saudi Arabian Government's desire to have their 560,000 Western guests leave their country as quickly as possible, created an opportunity for logistics excellence. Simply said, the scope of the retrograde problem, along with the speed

---

[3] Ibid., pp. 4-8. Concerning the M1 to M1A1 upgrade, many of the Army and Marine Corps' main battle tanks that were sent to theater were the "straight" M1 version with the 105mm main gun. The German made 120mm main gun that was placed on the then-newly produced M1A1 was a much better cannon overall, with more armor penetrating capability and more than one-half as much greater range. Developed and coordinated by Army Material Command, a plan was devised to replace all 105mm cannons on M1s with the new 120mm cannon, effectively turning the M1 into an M1A1. This model upgrade "swap-out line", located at the Port of Ad Dammam and operated by Army Material Command, modified all 948 tanks needing the "upgrade" ahead of schedule and approximately 25% below budget.

required to complete the retrograde by both U.S. and Saudi Governments, made Desert Farewell an unprecedented logistics challenge. Desert Farewell was certainly not indicative of the brigade level redeployments that are now seen with units supporting Operation Enduring Freedom (OEF) in Afghanistan or the former Operation Iraqi Freedom (OIF)—now Operation New Dawn—in Iraq. Units supporting OEF, for example, simply fall in on equipment of the unit they are replacing. For OIF, American equipment that was not sold or given to the New Iraqi Government was retrograded over a two-year period as forward operating bases (FOBs) ceased operations. Conversely, Desert Storm service members and their equipment had to leave as quickly as possible, beginning at least three weeks earlier than originally planned and working straight through until completion. Undaunted by the task at hand, military logisticians of the 22d Support Command made the redeployment happen, redeploying a daily average of 5,500 service members daily, and retrograding in excess of 1.2 million tons of material approximately six months ahead of schedule.[4]

Logistics preparation for Desert Storm combat operations (Desert Shield), as well as the redeployment/retrograde actions during Desert Farewell, were unprecedented in scope and speed. The importance of the logistics and sustainment capability of the United States military during the preparation phase was critical to the success of the

---

[4]Not many senior leaders at the time, on both the civilian and military sides, could fathom the extent of the redeployment/retrograde task after Desert Storm combat operations. The physical moving of men and materiel was the easy part of the equation in many respects. As an example, contracts had to be let for the construction of washracks to clean the soon to be retrograded military equipment to meet U.S. Department of Agriculture import standards. To go along with these washracks, the Corps of Engineers constructed a 4.8 million square foot concrete, partially covered, and secured area to keep the cleaned equipment sterile—and safeguarded—as it awaited its assigned ship for transportation back to its home station in the United States or Germany. All this was done while equipment and supplies were brought back to the Port of Ad Dammam from various points in the Iraqi, Kuwaiti, and Saudi Arabian Deserts, and as over 5,000 Soldiers, Sailors, Airman, and Marines were leaving daily. The raw numbers are mind-boggling; the retrograded ammunition alone weighed in excess of 250,000 tons and was valued at approximately four billion dollars—pound for pound more expensive than the Navy's largest aircraft carrier of the day, the U.S.S. Abraham Lincoln. See Pagonis, 11-14.

operation. Likewise, the success of an efficient, quick redeployment of service members and retrograde of their equipment was critical to retaining the good will that the United States had forged up to that point during the deployment to Southwest Asia, not only with the Saudi Arabian Royal Family, but with the Arab World as a whole.

As impressive as the preparation for and redeployment from Operation Desert Storm were from a logistics viewpoint, the sustainment of maneuver forces during combat operations was equally as notable and critical to the success of the overall mission. In an operation unprecedented in size, complexity, and logistics responsiveness, the sustainment plan for Desert Storm called for a series of logistics (sustainment) bases built *forward* of advancing U.S. forces as they flanked, then pursued and destroyed, the enemy in the western Iraqi desert. LTG Gus Pagonis, commander of the 22nd Theater Support Command (22nd SUPCOM) and responsible for all Coalition Force logistics for Operation Desert Storm, would not allow logistics/sustainment to be the weak link in the Desert Storm combat chain. Logistics failure at any level—particularly on ground at the operational and tactical level of war—was simply not an option. His intent was to have enough stocks of class I (food and water), III (fuel) and V (ammunition), along with the transportation assets required to move them, pre-positioned to sustain combat operations for the VII Corps and XVIII Airborne Corps *before* ground combat operations began on 24 February 1991. Thus, logistics base (log base) 'Charlie' (in support of XVIII Airborne Corps) and 'Echo' (in support of VII Corps) were established, stocked and prepared to support ground combat operations by 20 February 1991.

In an unprecedented plan to support two Corps elements in the attack, these logistics bases were initially established well into Iraq, approximately 70 miles northwest of each Corps' respective attack position in the Saudi Arabian Desert and in front of—as was then called in Air-Land Battle doctrine terminology—the FLOT (forward line of troops). The operation began with log bases Charlie and Echo established as well as map and ground reconnaissance conducted with locations identified for a series of subsequent log bases positioned further into Iraq. As each Corps pursued the Iraqi military, logisticians would "leap-frog" stocks from one log base to the next location, establishing a subsequent log base for continued support.[5] The previous ("moved from") logistics base would then be used largely as a EPW (enemy prisoner of war) holding area. Had the conflict continued for an extended period of time, XVIII Airborne Corps would have been supplied by logistics bases Oscar and Romeo, with VII Corps supplied by logistics bases Hotel and November.

At the beginning of the ground war on 24 February, Log base Charlie and Echo each had more than adequate stocks to sustain their respective supported Corps. On-hand quantities of selected stocks included enough food and water for 29 days, fuel for 5.2 days, and ammunition for 45 days. When the cease-fire took affect about four days later, Charlie and Echo still contained *at least* as much stocks as they held four days previous. With a secure rear area and virtually unimpeded lines of communication, each log base contained food and water for 29 days, fuel for 5.6 days, and ammunition for 65 days; a clear indicator that the sustainment plan became more efficient as time moved on. This is an astonishing feat, considering that—for example—VII and XVIII Corps'

---

[5] Given the length of the Desert Storm ground war—100 hours—only Logbases Charlie and Echo were established and used. However, had the ground conflict lasted longer, successive logistics bases were to be established using LTG Pagonis' "90-Mile Rule", stating that log bases would not be separated more than 90 miles, thought to be the maximum distance a given supply convoy could drive, round trip, given time required to unload their stocks and the desert driving conditions. See Pagonis, 146.

combined fuel consumption was over 4.4 million gallons daily (approximately 980 tanker

loads), with their ammunition consumption almost 14,000 tons a day.[6]

As the numbers indicate, the amount of men, equipment and material needed to

sustain a 560,000 member military force is of considerable size. However, pure size does

not take into account the professional attributes also required for victory in combat.

Aggressiveness, initiative, ingenuity and tactical patience do not only apply to maneuver

forces; the same traits are absolutely essential for sustainment success on the battlefield.

LTG Pagonis' forward positioning of log bases was a perfect example of these traits.

However, along with the overall reduction in the size of the military that began during

the Summer of 1991, the number of logistics forces were reduced as well. With this

reduction came an ever increasing dependence on, or simply use of, commercially

contracted civilian logistics providers beginning with Somalia in 1993, then continuing

on to the Balkans beginning in 1994, and Operations Enduring Freedom and Iraqi

Freedom, beginning in 2002 and 2003, respectively. This begs the questions: what

logistics forces were cut causing this need of contracted logistics forces?

Force Structure Cuts

In the period following Desert Storm, the United States military experienced

significant force structure cuts. The forcing function for what was to become a smaller

military was the "world order" at the time. By the Summer of 1991, the military threat

that was the Warsaw Pact had all but disintegrated with the political and economic

implosion of the Soviet Union in 1990. Also, the United States and its coalition partners

("coalition" more for a show of unity than out of tactical necessity) defeated what was

thought to be one of the world's preeminent military forces in Iraq using 37 days of air

---

[6] Pagonis, 147.

strikes followed by a 100-hour ground war. For American politicians and other leaders touting a world peace dividend and looking for savings to "add" cash to U.S. coffers, the military was a prime target. Taking a macro view of active duty military end strength at the end of each fiscal year, there was an overall decline in end strength numbers from 30 September 1990 (with an all service active duty population of 2,046,144) to 30 September 2010 (with an all service active duty population of 1,421,354). During the period, active duty end strength decreased by an aggregate of 624,790 service members.[7]

Using Army-specific numbers as an example, data for the same time period allows a comparison of the total active Army population (including logisticians, as logistics units are a commodity consumer that must be sustained as well) versus the number of Army logisticians on active duty. As depicted by the Soldier population graphs and their associated trend lines in Figure 2-1, the number of logisticians in the Army has decreased at a much slower rate as compared to the total Soldier population of the Army during this twenty year period. A review of the same chart reveals an almost flat trend line for the number of active Army logisticians, while the trend line for the total Active Army Soldier population shows a decidedly downward bent.[8] Using two fiscal years worth of data points as an example, on 30 September 1990 the Army had 732,403 Soldiers on active duty, 133,874 of which were logisticians, equating to approximately 18 percent of the total active duty Soldier population. On 30 September 2010 the Army had 566,045 Soldiers on active duty, 128,701 of which were logisticians, equating to

---

[7] Rod Hafemeister, "Who Is To Blame for the 'Too Small' Military?" http://rodhafemeister.wordpress.com/2008/04/28/whose-to-blame-for-the-too-small- military (accessed online 5 April 2011).

[8] Figures provided by Major Robert W. Erdman, U.S. Army G1 (Director, Personnel Strength and Analysis Forecasting) to the Author, 9 March 2011; information in author's possession.

approximately 23 percent of the active duty Army force. Once again using raw numbers, the total Army population was cut by 22.7 percent, while the logistician-specific Soldier population decreased 3.9 percent over the same twenty year period.

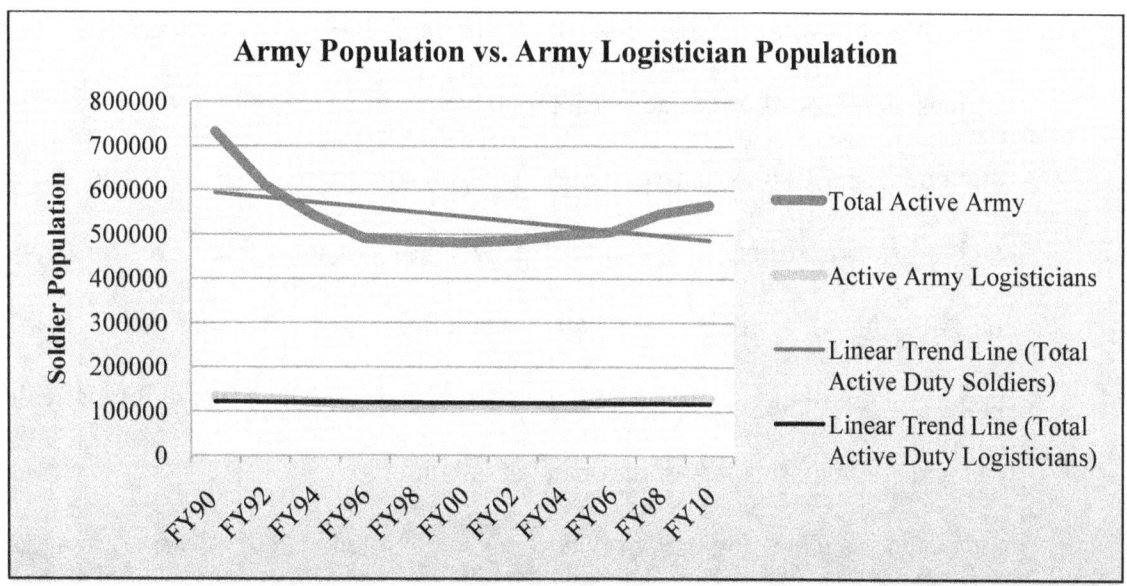

Figure 2-1

	Total Active Army	Active Army Logisticians	Percentage of Logisticians in the Active Army
FY90	732403	133874	18.3
FY92	610450	128634	21.1
FY94	541343	121151	22.4
FY96	491103	113698	23.1
FY98	483880	112749	23.3
FY00	482000	111109	23.1
FY02	486456	110348	22.7
FY04	498543	112835	22.6
FY06	505402	120626	23.9
FY08	547000	124233	22.7
FY10	566045	128701	22.7

Table 2-1

This "raw number" analysis indicates that, by percentage of total population, there is more logistics capability in the Army now than there was at the end of in September of 1990. Although significant force structure cuts were a reality for most of the Army, in particular infantry and armor units, logistics organizations were largely spared the extent of cuts suffered by their combat arms brethren.

Current Logistics Capability

Regardless of the coalition country or particular supported service—U.S. Army, Marines, Navy, Air Force, and our interagency partners as well—the Army is the component service ("executive agency") responsible for most strategic and all operational level logistics in Afghanistan and Iraq (as well as tactical level logistics for Army and non-Army units). There is no indication that a future conflict would call for a different support relationship. Consequently, the state of Army logistics capability is critical to all U.S. and coalition services during combat operations.

Once again using the Army as an example, the logisticians versus total force data depicted in this chapter shows that there is more uniformed ground logistics capability now than there was at the height of Desert Storm. In addition to having a numerical logistics advantage as opposed to the force of Desert Storm vintage, the Army is now logistically structured with modularity in mind. In the Summer of 2007, the Army began an overall restructuring to better utilize available resources (units, Soldiers, and equipment). Logistics units were a huge part of this restructuring, with the focus not placed upon habitual support to a particular unit, but with the capability to deploy with and sustain another maneuver unit, filling any particular mission-caused logistics gap that may exist in their particular support infrastructure.[9] As such, logistics units are not necessarily tied to a particular supported maneuver unit at the operational level and are

---

[9] First hand author account. At the time of this move to modularity, the author was G3 Chief of Plans, 13th Corps Support Command (now called the 13th Expeditionary Sustainment Command), Fort Hood, Texas, and involved in the modularity driven change of the 13th COSCOM to the 13th ESC.

able to be "plugged and played" into larger organizations to meet the sustainment and mission requirements of the supported unit. Although uncommon, logistics units can be mission-tailored at the tactical level as well.

Modularity has accomplished what it was designed to do—make more efficient use of our uniformed logisticians. Regardless of what level of warfare is concerned, adequate uniformed logistics forces and infrastructure exist to support our maneuver forces. There is also unity of command and unity of effort. In a combat theater, all logistics forces fall under the operational control (OPCON) of the deployed expeditionary sustainment command (ESC) headquarters. Just as, for example, there is one air component commander and one land component commander, the ESC commander (a brigadier general) is responsible directly to the land component commander for all logistics and sustainment operations in theater.

In addition to military supporters, civilian contracted logisticians must be included in any discussion of logistics capability. The U.S. military has set a precedence for using contractors on the battlefield, and chapter three of this document discusses historical uniformed versus civilian contracted force ratios. However, the current logistics capability in Iraq and Afghanistan is approaching a 1:1 force ratio as compared to uniformed military forces; for every Soldier, Marine, Airman or Sailor, there is one civilian contractor to work beside him.[10]

---

[10] Congressional Budget Office. "Contractor Support of U.S. Operations in Iraq," http://www.cbo.gov/ftpdocs/96xx/doc9688/MainText.3.1.shtml (accessed online 4 April 2011).

Logistics Capability Gap?

Returning to Figure 2-1, the Army, where the responsibility lies for logistics support for both Operation Iraqi Freedom/New Dawn and Operation Enduring Freedom, clearly has adequate logistics infrastructure on hand to support the required maneuver forces. To clarify the point, a 2005 Congressional Budget Office study determined that the United States military had the manpower and could perform sustainment tasks in Iraq and Afghanistan for the same costs as the current Logistics Civil Augmentation Program (LOGCAP) contract.[11] However, apparently not all uniformed logistics forces are being used. As will be discussed in detail in chapter three of this thesis, due largely to mandated military force caps and a consistent "mission creep" during combat operations, civilian contractors are fulfilling mission sets that in previous conflicts were the purview of military logisticians. In light of the 4 April 2004 contractor "walkout" discussed in the introduction of this thesis, this contractor assumption of responsibilities *en masse* leads to another question: will contractors be willing to go to a fight in a non-permissive environment? In other words, since the U.S. Department of Defense has placed many of its sustainment eggs in the contractor basket, does a capability gap exist based not upon what contractors are able to do, but rather what they are *not willing* to do?

---

[11] "Contractor Support of U.S. Operations in Iraq."

CHAPTER 3: HOW DID WE GET THERE?

.... Although there is historic precedence for contracted support to our military forces, I am concerned by our current level of dependency...[1]
-Secretary of Defense Robert M. Gates

In a 24 January 2011 memorandum to the service secretaries, Secretary Gates stated that there is a historical link between the United States military and their use of contractors. However, over the past decade of combat operations, this contracted arrangement has grown from being a force multiplier to a to a default force of "first option". Politically driven and mandated force caps placed on the military during combat operations, combined with the consistent "mission creep" in the form of subsequent missions the military is given, are but two factors that have added to American military's addiction to civilian sustainment contractors to the point that civilian contractual support has become a mainstay of U.S. military contingency operations.

Civilians on the Battlefield: Contractors vs. Military Force Ratios

The U.S. military's use of contractors on the battlefield has indeed been established throughout history. Over the past 235 years, civilian contractors have served alongside military uniformed service members and government employees, with their missions running the gamut from completing daily menial tasks to operating complicated transportation nodes. However, as depicted in Figure 3-1, the Defense Department's current use of contractors on the battlefield has reached unprecedented levels when compared to their supported uniformed counterparts.[2]

---

[1] U.S. Congress. House and Senate. Commission on Wartime Contracting in Iraq and Afghanistan. *Second Interim Report to Congress.* 113th Cong., 1st sess., February 24, 2011.

[2] Figure 3-1 and associated raw data at Table 3-1 originated from this CBO source as well. Congressional Budget Office. "Contractor Support of U.S. Operations in Iraq," http://www.cbo.gov/ftpdocs/96xx/doc9688/MainText.3.1.shtml (accessed online 4 April 2011).

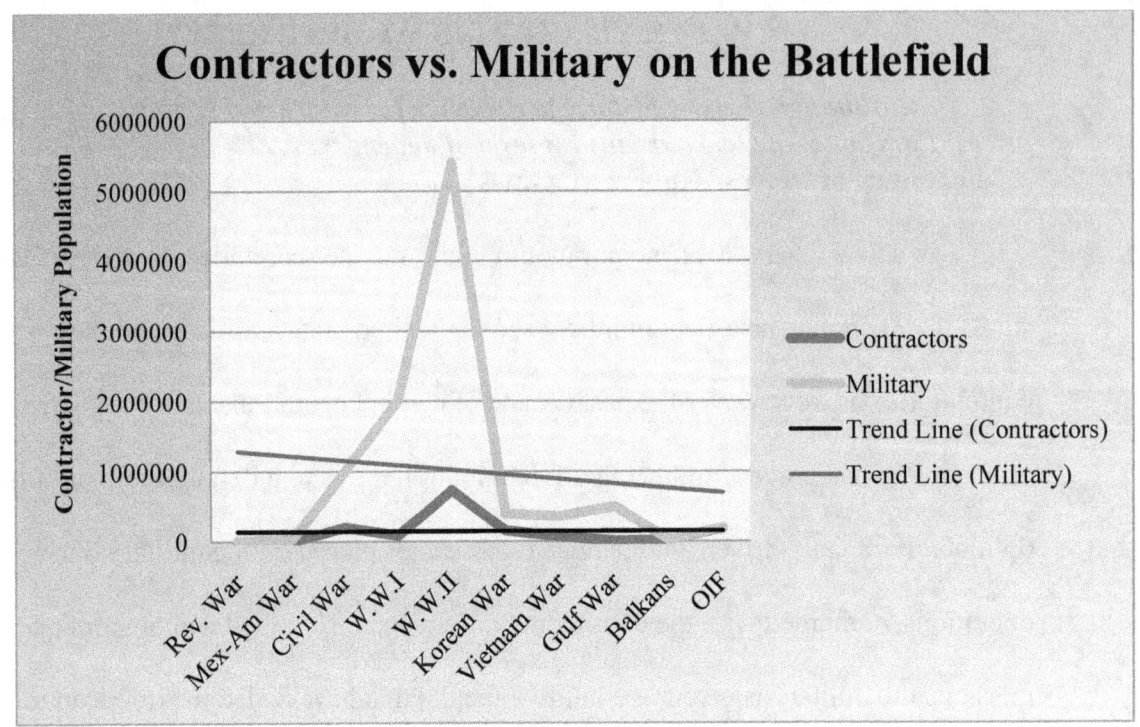

Figure 3-1

Raw Data (Including Force Ratio Calculations)

Conflict	Contractor	Military	Estimated Ratio of Contractor to Military Personnel
Revolutionary War	2,000	9,000	1 to 4.5
War of 1812	n.a.	38,000	n.a
Mexican-American War	6,000	33,000	1 to 5.5
Civil War	200,000	1,000,000	1 to 5.0
Spanish-American War	n.a.	35,000	n.a.
World War I	85,000	2,000,000	1 to 23.5
World War II	734,000	5,400,000	1 to 7.4
Korean War	156,000	393,000	1 to 2.5
Vietnam War	70,000	359,000	1 to 5
Gulf War	9,000	500,000	1 to 56
Balkans	20,000	20,000	1 to 1
OIF (JUL 2007)	190,000	200,000	.9 to 1
OEF (MAR 2011)	55,000	71,000	.8 to 1

Table 3-1

Analysis of the graph and associated data on the preceding page depicts two significant points. First, contractors have always been part of the "combined arms team"; their use was certainly not a twentieth century development. Secondly, the nearly 1 to 1 ratio of contractors to supported uniformed personnel during Operation Iraqi Freedom and Operation Enduring Freedom is significantly higher than it has been for any other conflict in American history, with the exception of operations in the Balkans.

During their highpoint in the late 1990s, U.S. military operations in the Balkans with its 1:1 contractor to supported military ratio foreshadowed how reliant the U.S. military would become on contracted support for military operations. Although only supporting a force of approximately 20,000 military service members, contracted support for operations in the Balkans was the template for future sustainment design. The Logistics Civil Augmentation Program (LOGCAP) contract began in earnest for support of military operations in the Balkans. Renamed the Balkans Support Contract in 1997, it has been the business test bed and contractual framework for what is now being used for contractor-provided support to operations in Iraq and Afghanistan.

As has been previously identified in this document, the United States Army—the component service responsible for all logistics in Iraq and Afghanistan—has more uniformed logisticians now than it did while supporting over twice the number of troops during the height of Operation Desert Storm (*see Figure 2-1 and Table 2-1*). Also, the United States military currently has almost a 1 to 1 contractor to supported service member force ratio (*see Figure 3-1 and Table 3-1)*. Consequently, the obvious question is "why does the military have a seemingly over-abundant group of supporting contractors, while concurrently having a higher percentage of the force serving as uniformed logisticians?"

Why Contracted Logistics?

The answer to the "why does the U.S. military have logistics contractors" question posed above must be divided into two different segments—how sustainment contracting became so deeply ingrained in the military and how it *remains* so deeply ingrained in the military.

The excessive use of contractors began with U.S. involvement in the Balkans. Originally hired to build base camps, the contracted company's initial task was purely "creature comforts" oriented, building "hard-stand" troop billets and dining facilities (with three hot meals daily) to get Soldiers and Marines out of tents in time for the harsh Balkan winter.[3] The company actively pursued other business "opportunities", capitalizing on the Defense Department's desire to reduce troop levels in the Balkans.[4] The contractors proved that the more they were hired to do, the less support forces the U.S. military would have to deploy. In less than two years, this creature comforts mission evolved into military vehicle maintenance, laundry services and uniform repair services as well as selected transportation operations, to include A/DACG (arrival/departure airfield control group) operations to process arriving and departing military personnel and their equipment. The contractors excelled at virtually every mission for which they were hired. Through actively searching for and hiring the right mix of recently separated and retired military officers and senior non-commissioned officers as managers, as well as civilian blue-collar experts in whatever career field they

---

[3] Hammes, T.X. "Private Contractors in Conflict Zones: The Good, the Bad, and the Strategic Impact." *Strategic Forum* (November 2010): 1-3.

[4] The author has purposely omitted the name of the contracted corporation.

needed, there was seemingly no mission they could not complete. The company's

performance evaluations were overwhelmingly positive.[5] After Operation Noble Anvil

(the air campaign against Bosnian Serb forces) was complete and peacekeeping

operations under the Kosovo Force (KFOR) began, the contractors were firmly

entrenched as an "option of first choice" for the United States military. For the first time

in history, there was a 1 to 1 ratio between civilian contractors and their supported

military force. Empowered by success, the relationship between sustainment contractors

and the U.S. military continued to build upon the foundation that was set in the Balkans.

The working partnership that began out of a need for quick and efficiently built shelter

for Soldiers and Marines in Bosnia evolved to what it is today—a marriage of necessity

and convenience—through a variety of paths, namely *political necessity, speed of

business*, and *professional ambiguity*.

Political necessity would outwardly seem to be an unusual motivation for a

government to remain involved in a contractual (business) agreement. However,

sustainment contracting in support of Operation Enduring Freedom and Operation Iraqi

Freedom/New Dawn provided a means to this "political necessity" end. First, contracted

sustainment troops are not counted under politically-mandated force structure/personnel

ceilings. Operations Enduring and Iraqi Freedom/New Dawn have always operated

under a strict military and government civilian personnel force structure ceiling. This

"cap" resulted in an almost maniacal management of forces—at the highest level—in

each theater of war. In some cases, elements moving into their respective combat zones

from Kuwait were not called forward until 21 days prior to the unit they were replacing

---

[5] As a Task Force primary staff member on two different military operations in the Balkans, the author was involved in quarterly evaluations of the Balkan Support Contract.

was to leave theater. Dependent on the political pain DoD was feeling at a given time, incoming senior commanders were not allowed to bring their staffs into the combat zone prior to the main body arrival of their unit. This strict adherence to the personnel cap continued regardless of tactical necessity. Military members on the ground were closely managed at the "eaches" level, to include individual rest and relaxation time. As the military recognized the need to expand its combat responsibilities to include stabilization and reconstruction, so did it recognize the need for more "tip of the spear" Soldiers. Consequently, the Department of Defense chose to maintain as many combat/maneuver units as possible under its end-strength caps. This solved the immediate problem of a lack of combat forces, but immediately exacerbated the problem of a lack of sustainment forces, a problem that was already at a critical stage in some areas. Thus, contingency contracting in Afghanistan and Iraq was increased as sustainment forces were replaced by combat/maneuver forces, with the Department of Defense contracting for much of what were once considered "core competency" sustainment tasks. This combination of increased mission load combined with the military's acceptance of a loss—albeit only during deployments—of organic capability opened a door through which a multitude of contractors were more than willing to pass.[6]

There is a second aspect to this "political necessity": the political impact of ongoing operations. As discussed in the previous section, arguably the greatest attribute of sustainment contractors is that they reduce the uniformed logistician requirement by replacing them with civilian contracted personnel. To go into detail using the 2007-2008 surge of forces in Iraq as an example, at the height of American troop strength in Iraq, the Department of Defense claimed that it had approximately 163,900 contractors fulfilling a

---

[6] *Second Interim Report to Congress*, 13.

variety of roles in Iraq.[7] By percentage, approximately 35 percent (or 57,365 civilians) of those contractors were part of the Logistics Civil Augmentation Program (LOGCAP) contract, providing a range of logistics and sustainment operations (transportation/distribution missions, maintenance services, arrival/departure airfield control operations, and "multi-class" storage sites for a variety of supplies) to OIF forces.[8] Proponents of sustainment contracting would argue that had those 57,365 contracted civilians not been working for the government, then 57,365—a force equal to about two Army Divisions—Soldiers, Marines, Sailors and Airmen would have had to take their place on the battlefield. Providing the additional two divisions worth of uniformed manpower would likely have required additional Reserve forces activations, certainly not a politically viable alternative to national elected leaders who want to keep their jobs for an additional term. Additionally, many of these 57,000+ contractors were "transportation specialists" (truck drivers) that functioned daily in what the military defines as a combat role. Drivers drove (and continue to drive) the main and alternate supply routes of Iraq and Afghanistan subjecting themselves to both improvised explosive devices and direct fire, taking casualties just as heavily as their military counterpart on the same convoys suffer. By the end of 2009, there were an estimated 630 deaths and almost 14,000 wounded sustainment contractors as a result of attacks on logistics elements in Iraq and Afghanistan.[9] As distasteful as it may seem, for political purposes these casualties were non-existent and had no impact on any discussion

---

[7] Hammes, 3-4.

[8] "Contractor Support of U.S. Operations in Iraq."

[9] Exact contractor casualties can be difficult to determine. Contractor casualties are tracked by the Department of Labor as opposed to the Department of Defense. Hammes, 1-4.

concerning the "human toll" of the Global War on Terrorism/Overseas Contingency Operations. Soldier deaths get reported; contractor deaths generally do not.

The tyranny of "I have to have it now", which can also be referred to as the *speed of business,* is another critical factor in why the use of sustainment contracts has continued. Large, industrial service-providing corporations that are accustomed to dealing with the U.S. Government, such as any of the prime contractors for the LOGCAP contract, have extensive resources at their disposal and many times are not bound by the same planning and resource constraints as their military logistician counterparts. The contractors holding the LOGCAP contract are very responsive. With the extensive salaries paid to hire "the best of the best available", their managers and workers are very capable, generally able to respond to major changes in differing and/or additional task orders ("changes of mission") more efficiently than a bureaucratic military is capable. For example, in preparation for the surge of U.S. forces into Iraq, an entirely new combat outpost (COB) had to be built in the Iraqi eastern desert to house the Army forces required for the surge operation. The soon to be named COB HAMMER, positioned approximately 70 miles east of Baghdad, had to be prepared to house two of the three brigades of the 3d Infantry Division, the Division headquarters, plus a two battalions worth of combat enablers and have space for the division (-) equipment—within 30 days. The scope of the problem, particularly considering the timeframe required, posed a significant problem to the military planners. The building of the COB was certainly within the capabilities of Army engineers, Navy Construction Battalions, or the Air Force "Red Horse" engineer teams, but they were not available in Iraq in the right quantities to allow them to continue their current respective "high priority" missions (such as rebuilding roads, water treatment plants, and other Iraqi infrastructure) as well as begin a new, large-in-scope project that had to be completed within thirty days. Additionally, CONUS (CONtinental United States) based Army, Air Force and Navy engineer teams were available and not yet deployed to Iraq, but were not considered at the time a personnel cap waiver was obtained for the surge operation, and thus were not included in "boots on the ground" (BOG) calculations to support the surge. Regardless, had the CONUS based engineer teams been included on the personnel cap waiver, the likelihood of any of the units and their equipment being able to deploy to Iraq *and* have the COB built within thirty days seemed like a dubious proposition. However, the prime LOGCAP contractor was able to begin the building process almost immediately. They re-arrange their internal priorities for a selected workforce already in Iraq, flew in structural engineers, plumbers, electricians, and initial materials from the U.S. within 72 hours, and began constructing facilities within 96 hours. The COB was complete, ready to be occupied on day thirty, as required.[10] Arguably, had the surge into Iraq not been so time dependent, but rather conditions dependent, U.S. forces in Iraq would not have had to rely upon contractors to complete a mission that military engineer elements were able to accomplish. Once again, the "I want it now" mentality seized the day. The building of COB HAMMER was not the only time that contractors stepped up to the plate in Iraq (and presumably Afghanistan) and saved the day, but it may very well be the largest—in scope—"off the cuff" operation. Previous to COB HAMMER, the contractor in Iraq changed supported locations, supply stockage objectives, and convoy procedures on very little notice and with great success. The point can be made that American military

---

[10] Firsthand experience. The author was on the 13th Sustainment Command staff prior to, during and after "the surge" in Iraq and involved in the planning process for the building of COB HAMMER.

leaders and planners were lulled into a reliance upon a contractor that seemingly never failed a mission, further perpetuating the "I want it now" mentality.

The last reason for the U.S. military's continued partnership with contractors is one of *professional ambiguity*. Simply put, the Department of Defense sometimes operates vicariously through sustainment contractors in order to coordinate sustainment in certain situations. On occasion, contractors are able to accomplish tasks that the U.S. military forces cannot due to challenges posed by less than optimum relationships among neighboring countries. A case in point is providing for bulk fuel for forces supporting Operation Enduring Freedom. Due to tactical necessity and lessons learned from the insurgent attacks on Iraqi main and alternate routes in April of 2004, the U.S. military had to coordinate for additional ground lines of communication (supply routes) for bulk fuel to support forces inside of Afghanistan. Because of political sensitivities with one country versus another (such as India and Pakistan), it was almost impossible for any United States Government entity to coordinate an agreement between itself and India, Pakistan, Turkmenistan, and Afghanistan involving the transfer of interstate goods. At any given time at least two of the countries involved (once again, usually India and Pakistan) refused to be involved in any agreement that involved the "other" country. Consequently, organizing these supply routes and agreements with sub-contractors was given to an element of the Army's Acquisition Command. Acquisition Command—in turn—contracted with companies in each country, bypassing the need to broker an all-encompassing agreement with multiple countries in the region. Each contractor was then given a certain quantity of fuel to deliver to specific crossing points on the Afghani border at specific times, to be escorted to their final destination by U.S. forces. In essence, contractors did what the U.S. Government could not. To get their fuel through (and make a nice profit from the United States as well), contractors in each country were able to pay a "movement tax" to local tribal elders in remote parts of countries involved in order to pass through their respective areas. Additionally, fringe supporters of the Taliban and al Queda could not outwardly determine if fuel semi-trucks they may have seen passing their village were for internal consumption of the country they were in, or if they were to be used for another purpose (such as to support OEF forces). Once again, *professional ambiguity* allows contractors to arrange for sustainment of U.S. forces in an environment where it may not be possible for a U.S. sustainment command to operate openly.

These "paths" of *political necessity, speed of business*, and *professional ambiguity* have paved the way for a lengthy, in depth relationship between the Department of Defense and sustainment contractors. This contractual relationship began as a relatively simple contractual mission for the construction of billeting spaces and dining facilities for troops in the Balkans. Over the past decade and a half, the relationship has evolved into a contractual monster with over five billion dollars spent on a variety of sustainment operations normally accomplished by Army and Marine logistics units.[11]

Problem Set--Contracted Logistics in a Non-Permissive Environment

With the beginning of contractual support to U.S. forces in the Balkans, defense contractors (defense *sustainment* contractors in particular) have enjoyed a relatively safe working environment. In the Balkans, contractors worked in very permissive environment in support of peace-keeping or peace-making operations. Initial tasks

---

[11] "Contractor Support of U.S. Operations in Iraq."

involved building billets for Soldiers and Marines, running dining facilities and progressed slowly into additional base operations missions. Contractors rarely left their base camps in the Balkans and Kosovo while supporting operations there, and certainly were not targets when they did leave their respective cantonment areas. Although much more contractually robust at the outset of the operation as compared to the previous Balkans Support Contract and LOGCAP (version one), contractors in the opening phase of OIF still worked in a very permissive environment. They only operated in cleared areas behind U.S. lines. With the fall of the Iraqi Government about thirty days after combat operations, U.S. contractors were treated like conquering heroes by the Iraqi people, in the same manner as their uniformed military counterparts were treated.

However, with the influx of al Queda into Iraq, the tide of Iraqi opinion began to turn against Americans. As terrorist groups began to influence the Iraqi populace to either turn a blind eye on attacks against the United States and Coalition forces or to participate openly in similar attacks, casualties against military and sustainment contractors began to rise. These early al Qaeda-in-Iraq (AQ-I) influenced and supported attacks increased in frequency and severity, culminating on 4 April 2004 with a series of well coordinated attacks at several points on Coalition main and alternate supply routes across Iraq. In addition to severing vitally important ground lines of communication (LOCs), these attacks resulted not only in the deaths of several service members, but of civilian contractors as well. The effect of these attacks, combined with killing of four contractors in Fallujah less than a week previous, caused the largest U.S. defense contractor in the region to "blink" and reconsider its lucrative sustainment contract with the U.S. Government.

This contractual "blink" is the crux of the U.S. military's overreliance on sustainment contracting, and centers around the lack of willingness, rather than the lack of ability, of civilian contractors to support the military in a theater opening, non permissive environment similar to those described above and in the scenarios in the opening chapter of this thesis. Contractors came back "on line" approximately six days after the 4 April attacks. The only reason why the sustainment contractors came back on line at all was because of a guarantee of military support. This "guarantee" included a 1 to 5 "shooter" (gun truck/convoy protection platform) to contracted vehicle ratio per combat logistics patrol (convoy). Soldiers or Marines were to ride in the cabs of trucks as secondary shooters and, in many cases, there would be a requirement for combat engineer units to clear main and alternate supply routes immediately before contractor convoys departed for each convoy that went on the road (which on some days could be as much as 60 convoys a day). Compared to the current COIN operations in Iraq and Afghanistan, any hybrid conflict that the United States may become involved in would likely require fighting a much better equipped, possibly more determined enemy than the country faces now. Consequently, based upon prior experience when facing a "fighting enemy" in Iraq and Afghanistan, the security required by contractors in a hybrid warfare scenario may be more Soldier and Marine-resource intensive than the military can afford. Every Soldier, Marine, Sailor or Airman tasked to ride in a cab of a contracted, civilian vehicle takes that young warrior away from the military mission for which he was trained. Simply put, in a hybrid warfare scenario similar to ones described earlier in this thesis, military units would not have the manpower or time to devote the amount of resources required to fulfill contractor-required security requirements. However, with the current 1:1 contractor to military ratio, and, more insidiously, the easy reliance on contracted work, the U.S. may be forced to accept such limitations, ultimately reducing its ability to achieve its political-military objectives as fast as national or international policy-makers desire or the nation requires.

CHAPTER 4: RECOMMENDATIONS

Although there is historic precedent for contracted support to our military forces, ... The time is now—while lessons learned from recent operations are fresh—to institute the changes necessary to influence a cultural shift.[1]
-**Secretary of Defense Robert M. Gates**

Recommendations to fix the military's sustainment contract predicament must have a common goal of not making contractors the "default option" for sustainment support. Military sustainment contractors have done very well in what has essentially been an almost twenty year marketing campaign to convince the Department of Defense that they are indeed an indispensible resource on the battlefield. Likewise, changing the military's behavior concerning a much more limited and prudent use of sustainment contracting will involve just as much effort. To alleviate the contracting issue, the U.S. military should concentrate its efforts in three specific areas: using military logistics capability that resides in our military; leveraging emerging military capability; and realizing a that there is still a role for contractors in military support.

Use Current Military Sustainment Capability

Per capita, the United States military now has more sustainment capability than it held during the height of Operation Desert Storm. As an example, the Army now consists of approximately 23 percent logisticians, while at the end of Operation Desert Storm, the logistician population never exceeded 18 percent as a percentage of the total supported population. However, the U.S. military now has more contracted logisticians than it has ever had in its history—a ratio approaching one contractor for every supported serviceman. The practice of using sustainment contractors as the choice of "first option" must cease for two reasons. First, it is fiscally irresponsible to use

---

[1] *Second Interim Report to Congress.*

contracted assets when the U.S. military has the expertise to do the job, particularly in an era of ever declining defense budgets. In support of Operation Iraqi Freedom from March 2003 through September 2007, the Department of Defense spent in excess of $22 billion for the Logistics Civil Augmentation Program contract alone (and this is a very tenuous figure, and may be larger if all base construction costs are placed under the LOGCAP contract in addition to standard logistics functions). By itself, the LOGCAP contract accounts for approximately 29% of the $76 billion spent by the DoD on OIF related contractual obligations during the same time period.[2] Second, the military is losing its institutional logistics/sustainment savvy. In many cases, sustainment contractors are relied upon as the subject matter expert in a particular sustainment field. Their contractual organization mirrors that of a military logistics organization and their hired leaders/managers are generally considered some of the very best in their respective fields. Consequently, this has resulted in military logisticians at certain levels not knowing how to accomplish specific tasks because those logisticians have entered the force and have been professionally developed in an era of contracting when the contractor was responsible for such tasks. This reliance upon contractors is evident at pre-deployment training locations such as the National Training Center (NTC) at Fort Irwin, California. Although primarily geared to ground operations, units from all services train at the NTC prior to deploying to Iraq and Afghanistan. The Army and Marine Captain and Major level logisticians are tactically adept, but lack the sustainment planning skills required of their jobs. It is quite common to find a relatively young-in-career officer who does not know how to plan sustainment operations fully or develop

---

[2] "Contractor Support of U.S. Operations in Iraq."

60

something as simple as a sustainment matrix (to place it in a combat arms perspective, not being able to develop a sustainment matrix to a logistician is on par with an infantry officer not being able to develop a sector sketch).[3] This lack of training must be fixed as well. These young officers will grow to become not-so-young sustainment battalion commanders who are incapable of conducting the most basic of sustainment tasks, but now responsible for developing junior officers and supporting potentially thousands of other servicemen.

Use Emerging Capability

One emerging capability that would indeed transfer several sustainment contractor "owned" tasks as well as provide the military a guaranteed aerial port foothold in a non-permissive environment is the Air Force's Joint Task Force-Port Opening (JTF-PO). The JTF-PO's mission is to "provide a joint expeditionary capability to rapidly establish and operate a port of debarkation and conduct cargo handling and movement operations to a forward node, facilitating port throughput in support of combatant commander executed contingencies."[4] JTF-PO capabilities are significant and include: port of debarkation (POD) distribution and network assessment; POD opening and operations; establishing POD communications, ITV (in transit visibility) and RFID (radio frequency identification) networks; cargo handling/movement; and movement control synchronization. Besides returning this port opening task to its rightful military owner,

---

[3] First-hand knowledge. The author commanded the only deployable battalion at the National Training Center and deployed assets to both OIF and OEF. Consequently, the author's battalion trained subordinate elements during several different NTC rotations. The CPT-MAJ logistics officer "trend" referenced was noted in post-rotation AARs of several units.
[4] Scott Zippwald, Discussion concerning the Air Force's Joint Task Force-Port Opening capability. Joint Forces Staff College, Norfolk, VA, 5 April 2011.

the Air Force's JTF-PO units would guarantee in transit visibility of cargo, which is an area where sustainment contractors have struggled.

Still a Role for Contractors

The roll that contractors should fill falls into two categories: tasks where the military lacks expertise, and areas where the military may not be as effective due to political sensitivities. Concerning the first point, contractual tasks should include what the military calls "low density mode of service" tasks. These low density MOSs—as they are called—are tasks that are important to a deployed Soldier, Marine, Sailor or Airman's well being, but generally performed by specialized, albeit low-in-quantity units. An example of a low density unit is a laundry and bath/clothing repair companies (all of which now reside in the Army Reserve). Having contractors fill this "low density" roll would augment the military's capability and eliminate the need for a continuous call-up of these scarce assets. The second type of tasks ripe for contractor action are any tasks involving the obtaining of and/or the transportation of commodities through countries or regions that may not want to do business with the United States Government or with one of their neighbors. As discussed in the previous chapter concerning the transportation of fuel into Afghanistan, sustainment contractors can still play a vital role in supporting the nation's combat operations through indirect sustainment action.

CHAPTER 5: CONCLUSION

As aptly stated by Field Marshall Erwin Rommel, "the battle is fought and decided by quartermasters before the shooting begins."[1] This statement alone shows the importance one of history's greatest, most tactically and operationally proficient military leaders placed on logistics (or sustainment, as it is now more commonly referred). However, if not given its due planning effort, sustainment—or more accurately, the lack of sustainment capability—will cause a military operation to fail. Ironically, this logistics failure was the primary downfall of Field Marshall Rommel's forces in the North African Campaign during World War II.

Logistics is like any other art and science—it must be studied. Logisticians must study warfare just as tirelessly as their maneuver/combat arms counterparts do. The types of warfare faced—high intensity conflict, counter insurgency warfare, and hybrid warfare—all have specific challenges that make them each part of a difficult sustainment problem to solve when planning to support U.S. military combatant forces; today's logisticians must know these problems and be prepared for them (albeit facing a downward knowledge trend as experience dwindles.)

A significant factor in U.S. preparation for sustainment of forces in combat is having the right type of logistics forces in which to help carry the fight to the enemy. The U.S. military now relies very heavily on a contracted force for combatant sustainment. In spite of the fact that, per capita, there are more uniformed logisticians now in the United States military than any other period in history, contractors supporting the sustainment of our forces in combat also constitute a proportionally greater subset of

---

[1] Rommel, 328.

the logistician population than any time in history, approaching a 1 to 1 ratio as compared to the military population they support. From relatively humble beginnings, sustainment contracting has become a multi-billion dollar business for contractors, in large part because the Department of Defense has allowed contracting to be the "the first among equals" in options for supporting its forces in combat. The Department of Defense must fix this sustainment status quo. As discussed in Chapter Four of this document, maximizing current sustainment capability, leveraging emergent sustainment capability and finding the "right fit" for contractors in strategic support of combat forces is critical to ensuring the success of future combat operations.

It is essential that the United States fix this "contractor heavy" approach to sustainment, as eventually the United States will become embroiled in a war that contractors will want no part of. As evidenced in April 2004 by the contractors "mass exodus" after taking—as compared to other combat actions—light casualties, civilian contractors may not run to the sound of the guns, but from them, when it comes to supporting U.S. maneuver forces in the next war.

BIBLIOGRAPHY

Bearor, Jeffrey. "Future of Conflict: Hybrid Threats in Complex Environments" for the
   Commanding General, Marine Corps Combat Development Command
   (25 April 2008): 1-4.

Cheng, Dean. "Chinese Views on Deterrence." *Joint Forces Quarterly* (January 2011):
   92-94.

Congressional Budget Office. "Contractor Support of U.S. Operations in Iraq,"
   http://www.cbo.gov/ftpdocs/96xx/doc9688/MainText.3.1.shtml
   (accessed online 4 April 2011).

Congressional Research Service. "Department of Defense Contractors in Iraq and
   Afghanistan: Background and Analysis,"
   http://fpc.state.gov/documents/organization/145569.pdf (accessed online 4 April
   2011).

Congressional Research Service. "Russian Natural Gas: Regional Dependence,"
   http://www.fas.org/sgp/crs/misc/RS22562.pdf (accessed online 10 March 2011).

Cunningham, Charles J. Office discussion concerning China. Joint Forces Staff College,
   Norfolk, VA, 4 January 2011.

Erdman, Robert W. Spreadsheet detailing the Army logistics population. Headquarters,
   Department of the Army, ACofS, G1, Washington, D.C., 10 March 2011.

Dickson, Keith. A Clash of Civilizations: Russia. TH 6116A Joint Advanced
   Warfighting School lecture, Norfolk, VA, January 5, 2011

Epstein, Gady and Robyn Meredith. "US Companies that Invest Big in China: American
   Companies Invest in China, Chasing Global Growth," *Forbes.Com* (5 July 2010),
   www.forbes.com/2010/07/05/us-investments-china-markets-emerging-markets-
   fdi.html (accessed online 8 March 2011).

Flournoy, Michelle A. and Shawn Brimely. "The Defense Inheritance: Challenges and
   Choices for the Next Pentagon Team," *The Washington Quarterly* (Autumn 2008):
   59-76.

Gates, Robert M. "A Balanced Strategy: Reprogramming the Pentagon for a New Age."
   Foreign Affairs (January/February 2009): 28-41.

Hammes, T.X. "Private Contractors in Conflict Zones: The Good, the Bad, and the
   Strategic Impact." *Strategic Forum* (November 2010): 1-14.

Hafemeister, Rod. "Who Is To Blame for the 'Too Small' Military?" http://rodhafemeister.wordpress.com/2008/04/28/whose-to-blame-for-the-too-small-military (accessed online 5 April 2011).

Hoffman, Frank G. "Hybrid Warfare and Challenges." *Joint Forces Quarterly* (October 2009): 34-39

Horowitz, Michael C. and Dan A. Shalon. "The Future of War and American Military Strategy." *Military Strategy* (Spring 2009): 300-317.

Howard, Michael. "Military Science in an Age of Peace." *RUSI: The Journal of the Royal United Services Institute, 119* (March 1974): 3-11.

International Military Forums. "International Military Forum: About Logistics Quotes," found online at http://www.military-quotes.com/forum/logistics-quotes-t511.html (accessed 11 March 2011).

Kissinger, Henry. "The U.S. Should Be Careful in Egypt," 1 February 2011, http://www.newsmax.com/TheWire/Kissinger-U-SCareful-Egypt/2011/02/01/id/384589#ixzz1EWFU3Le2 (accessed 20 February 2011).

Krepinevich, Andrew F. *7 Deadly Scenarios.* New York: Bantam Books, 2009.

_____. "The Future of U.S. Ground Forces: Challenges and Requirements." http://www.csbaonline.org (accessed 19 February 2011).

Kraus, Theresa L. and Frank N. Schubert, eds. *The Whirlwind War: The United States Army in Operation Desert Shield and Desert Storm.* Found online at http://www.history.army.mil/books/www/wwindx.htm (accessed 11 March 2011).

Lee, Don. "China Investments in the U.S. Up Sharply", *LA Times Online,* 4 March 2010 http://articles.latimes.com/2010/mar/04/business/la-fi-china-invest4-2010mar04 (accessed 9 March 2011).

McChrystal, Stanley A. "It Takes a Network: The New Frontline of Modern Warfare," www.foreignpolicy.com/ariticles/2011/02/22/it_takes_a_network (accessed online 7 March 2011).

McGrath, John J. "Occasional Paper 23-The Other End of the Spear: The Tooth-to-Tail Ratio (T3R) In Modern Military Operations." Fort Leavenworth: Combat Studies Institute Press, 2007.

Nagl, John. "Institutionalizing Adaptation: It's Time for a Permanent Army Advisor Corps," www.cnas.org/files/documents/.../Nagl_AdvisoryCorp_June07.pdf (accessed online 20 January 2010).

Oliker, Olga and Tanya Charlik-Paley, *Assessing Russia's Decline—Trends and Implications for the United States and the U.S. Air Force.* Santa Monica, CA: Rand Corporation, 2002.

Pagonis, William G. *Moving Mountains—Lessons in Leadership and Logistics from the Gulf War.* Boston: Harvard Business School Press, 1992.

Rommel, Erwin J.E. *The Rommel Papers.* Edited by Basil Henry Liddel Hart. New York: Harcourt, Brace and Company, 1953.

_____. *Infanterie greift an (Infantry Attacks)*, 1937.

Reuters. "Chinese Investment in the U.S.: $2 Trillion and Counting," http://blogs.reuters.com/india-expertzone/2011/03/02/chinese-investment-in-us-2-trln-and-counting/ (accessed 9 March 2011).

Rubin, Uzi. *The Rocket Campaign Against Israel During the 2006 Lebanon War.* Ramat Gan, Israel: Began-Sadat Center for Strategic Studies, 2007.

Shanker, Thom. "Warning Against Wars Like Iraq and Afghanistan", *New York Times Online,* 25 February 2011 http://www.nytimes.com/2011/02/26/world/26gates.html (accessed 9 March 2011).

Soloman, Jay. "U.S. Fears Tripoli May Employ Gas as Chaos Mounts," *The Wall Street Journal,* 24 February 2011.

The Army in World War Two. "The Red Ball Express." The JCS Group, http://www.jcs-group.com/military/war1941army/etoredball.html (accessed online 13 December 2010).

U.S. Congress. House and Senate. Commission on Wartime Contracting in Iraq and Afghanistan. *Second Interim Report to Congress.* 113th Cong., 1st sess., February 24, 2011.

U.S. Congress. Senate. Committee on the Armed Services. *The Department of Defense's Management of Costs Under the logistics Civil Augmentation Program (LOGCAP) Contract in Iraq.* 110th Cong., 1st sess., April 19, 2007.

U.S. Department of Defense. *Objective Assessment of Logistics in Iraq: DUSD (L&MR) And Joint Staff (JSJ4) Sponsored Assessment to Review the Effectiveness and Efficiency of Selected Aspects of Logistics Operations During Operation Iraqi Freedom (OIF).* Washington, D.C.: Government Printing Office, March 2004.

_____. *Joint Logistics Strategic Plan 2010-2014.* Washington, D.C.: Government Printing Office, 2010.

_____. *Joint Publication 1: Doctrine for the Armed Forces of the United States (Revision First Draft.* Washington, D.C.: Government Printing Office, 14 December 2010.

_____. *Joint Publication 1-02: Department of Defense Dictionary of Military and Associated Terms.* Washington D.C.: Government Printing Office, 31 December 2010.

_____. *Joint Publication 3-0: Joint Operations.* Washington, D.C.: Government Printing Office, 22 March 2010.

_____. *Objective Assessment of Logistics in Iraq.* Washington, D.C.: Government Printing Office, March 2004.

U.S. Director of National Intelligence. *Statement for the Record on the Worldwide Threat Assessment of the U.S. Intelligence Community for the Senate Committee on Armed Services,* March 10, 2011.

U.S. Joint Forces Command. *The Joint Operating Environment (JOE) 2010.* Suffolk, VA: United States Joint Forces Command, February 18, 2010.

Van der Heijden, Kees. *Scenarios: The Art of Strategic Communication.* Hoboken: John Wiley and Sons, 2005.

Veblen, Thorstein. "The Evolution of the Scientific Point of View." *The University of California Chronicle*, vol. 10, no. 4 (May 4, 1908), https://sites.google.com/site/thorsteinveblenmurillocruzdsc/artigos-selecionados-de-veblen/evolution (accessed online 29 March 2011).

von Clausewitz, Carl. *On War.* Edited and translated by Michael Howard and Peter Paret. New York: Alfred A. Knopf, 1976.

Winterford, David. A Clash of Civilizations: China. TH 6116B Joint Advanced Warfighting School lecture, Norfolk, VA, January 6, 2011.

Zakaria, Fareed. "The Future of American Power." *Foreign Affairs* (May/June 2008): 18-43.

Zippwald, Scott . Discussion concerning the Air Force's Joint Task Force-Port Opening capability. Joint Forces Staff College, Norfolk, VA, 5 April 2011.